Getting Through To Adults

James T. Dyet

ACCENT BOOKS
Denver, Colorado

ACCENT BOOKS
A division of Accent-B/P Publications, Inc.
12100 W. Sixth Avenue
P.O. Box 15337
Denver, Colorado 80215

Copyright © 1980 Accent-B/P Publications, Inc.
Printed in United States of America

Library of Congress Catalog Card Number: 79-53294

ISBN 0-89636-037-7

Second Printing 1981

Contents

"He who teaches the Bible is never a scholar; he is always a student."
                              —Anonymous

1 First Things First

In case you haven't heard it for a while, if ever, "Congratulations." For what? For becoming a member of a highly influential group — teachers of adults in Sunday School. And it doesn't matter whether you received your first teacher's manual twenty years ago or twenty minutes ago; you deserve the congratulations.

You see, as a teacher of adults, your influence is so great that it extends beyond time and reaches into eternity. Now, that's a staggering thought to get a grip on; so, in case you didn't take it all in the first time you read it, let me repeat it:

Your influence is so great that it extends beyond time and reaches into eternity.

Through your example and instruction it is highly possible that some adults will see their need of Christ as Saviour and will trust in Him. As a result, they will end up in Heaven instead of in Hell. And, hopefully, before they get there, they will have taken long strides in the Christian walk and contributed significantly to the fulfillment of the Great Commission. And think of the encouragement and guidance you can give to others who already know the Lord. Why, there's no limit to what God can do through your life and teaching ministry! The opportunity defies description!

But opportunity knocks; it doesn't break down the door. So prepare for its arrival.

Some teachers, I'm sad to say, have missed that big opportunity to be used of God to enrich the lives of others. Oh, they showed up for class Sunday by Sunday, but nothing much happened in terms of meaningful student response. Between the ringing of the first bell and the last it was just business as usual in the classroom. And after the last bell the students filed out, taking with them nothing but closed Bibles and half-read take-home Sunday School papers. How different things could have been with proper preparation on the part of those teachers!

Now, let me explain what kind of preparation I mean. It's the kind demonstrated by a great teacher in the Old Testament, whose name was Ezra. Charged with the awesome responsibility of giving spiritual instruction to the repatriated Jews who had returned to Jerusalem from the Babylonian Captivity, Ezra "prepared his heart to seek the law of the Lord, and to do it, and to teach in Israel statutes and judgments" (Ezra 7:10). Heart preparation, that's the most basic and most important preparation a teacher can make. There's no such thing as successful teaching without it. A teacher can attend the largest Sunday School convention in the country, sit in every available workshop, visit all the booths and fill a shopping bag with handouts and his head with ideas, but none of that can substitute for heart preparation.

God puts a heavy emphasis on the heart, because what goes on deep inside a person's silent world of thoughts and feelings will surely surface in his actions. Proverbs 23:7 explains, "For as he thinketh in his heart, so is he." Who knows, it may have been this verse of Scripture that offered the greatest persuasion to Ezra to prepare his heart for the momentous task he faced.

A PREPARED HEART TO SEEK GOD'S WORD

Ezra committed himself to "seek the law of the Lord." In doing so, he recognized a basic principle — if you plan to teach a subject, know the subject you plan to teach. I remember so clearly the longest day I ever spent in a classroom as a substitute teacher in the Altoona Area High School in Altoona, Pennsylvania. One of the art teachers had called in sick, and I was contacted to take his classes. I had subbed before in French and German, subjects with which I had fairly decent familiarity, but I knew absolutely nothing about art. Why, to this day, I can hardly draw a circle that doesn't look like a deformed football. The only reason why I agreed to "teach" art on that day of infamy was the insistence of the principal's office that my "just being there would help the students to stick to their work."

Well, after six hours of apologizing to students for not being able to respond to their questions with anything more brilliant than "I don't know," I felt that my contribution to their education was about as valuable as one cent mailed postage due to Washington, D.C. to help pay off the national debt. So, if you want to make a contribution to your adults' Christian education, prepare your heart, as Ezra prepared his to know God's Word.

This will cost you something. You may have to forego something that presently consumes quite a bit of your time in order to invest more time in the study of Scripture. Don't believe anyone who says Sunday School teaching doesn't require much of a person's time. That kind of talk reveals either dishonesty or ignorance of the facts. *Teaching that costs little will accomplish little.*

I heard somewhere about a teacher of adults who claimed that he didn't have to study his Bible in preparation for Sunday School. "I just show up for class, open my mouth, and the Lord fills it," he boasted. But, upon hearing his teacher's empty boast, a student countered, "And, when you hear what he says to us, it makes you wonder if that's the best the Lord can do!" You may be sure that little was accomplished in that adult class.

Ezra's intense desire to know the law of the Lord typifies the attitude that many of God's choicest servants of Bible history displayed. Moses, David, John the Baptist, and the Apostle Paul experienced aloneness with God in the wilderness before entering public ministry as God's appointed spokesmen. Even our Saviour kept His heart in tune with the Father by commencing a day of ministry with private communion with Him. If these great men and the God-Man took time for heart preparation, how can any teacher forego it?

There isn't any method of Bible study that is best for everyone. Some persons enjoy and profit from reading an entire book of the Bible at a time. Others prefer to read through a book of the Bible over a period of several days or weeks, checking carefully the context of each paragraph and chapter. A few feel obliged to cross-reference subjects and key words. Whatever suits you best is the method you should follow. The really important thing is to keep up persistent and consistent Bible study, meditating upon God's character, marvelous works, gracious resources, and righteous requirements. Attention should be paid to principles that can help you, and ultimately your students, to worship and serve God in a manner that pleases Him.

As I have studied the Scriptures through the years, I have been helped by the following questions:

• What is the central teaching of this passage of Scripture?

• How does this passage relate to the one that precedes it and to the one that follows it?

• What can I learn about God from this passage?

• What can I learn about human nature from this

passage?
- What does this passage reveal about me?
- How can this passage of Scripture help me to be a stronger, more effective Christian?
- What are my responsibilities, according to this passage? In regard to God? In regard to others?
- What other passages of Scripture seem to parallel this one?

These questions may be categorized under the four headings shown in the "Topics to Explore in a Scripture Passage" chart. Of course, you may find it more to your personal liking to add a few more headings. What is offered here is simply a guide for you to use with or without adaptations.

I want to emphasize that daily, personal Bible study will do more to equip you for your role as a teacher than anything else. There simply is no substitute for it, in spite of all the helps for teaching that are available today. When you seek God's Word with an intense desire to know Christ better and to get better acquainted with His will, you will bring a spiritual freshness and power to your teaching that adults long for.

A PREPARED HEART TO OBEY GOD'S WORD

Now, let's get back to Ezra. Not only did he prepare his heart to seek the law of the Lord, but also "to do it" (Ezra 7:10). As a dedicated priest and scribe, Ezra wanted to present a suitable example for the nation to follow. As we all know, people expect a teacher to practice what he teaches. They look for illustration of the truth in the teacher's life before they listen very intently to his instruction about the truth. Upon observing a teacher's consistent application of God's Word to his own life, students are far more eager to pattern their behavior after the precepts of Scripture.

TOPICS TO EXPLORE IN A SCRIPTURE PASSAGE

Context	God	Myself	Others
What is the central thought?	His character?	What am I like?	What does this passage teach about others?
What precedes this passage?	His resources?	What does God want me to become?	
What follows this passage?	His promises?		What are my duties toward others?
What are some related passages?	His requirements?	How can I become a stronger, more effective Christian?	
Who is speaking?			
To whom is this passage primarily addressed?			

Many centuries before Ezra assumed the role of Israel's teacher, Saul became Israel's first king. As a member of God's chosen race, Saul must have been aware of the high standard God had set for His people in Deuteronomy 10:12,13: "And now, Israel, what doth the Lord thy God require of thee, but to fear the Lord thy God, to walk in all his ways, and to love him, and to serve the Lord thy God with all thy heart and with all thy soul, To keep the commandments of the Lord, and his statutes." Furthermore, Deuteronomy 17:18,19 gave specific instructions to him and all future kings of Israel regarding their responsibility toward God's Word. "And it shall be, when he sitteth upon the throne of his kingdom, that he shall write him a copy of this law in a book out of that which is before the priests the Levites: And it shall be with him, and he shall read therein all the days of his life: that he may learn to fear the Lord his God, to keep all the words of this law and these statutes, to do them." Saul's responsibility, then, was precisely the same as Ezra's ambition—to seek the law of the Lord, and to do it.

But Saul failed miserably, and no amount of high-sounding pious talk or offering sacrifices could compensate for his failure to obey God. First Samuel 15 relates the sad story of how his disobedience disqualified him from continuing to reign over the nation. By divine commandment, Saul was supposed to slay the Amalekites and not spare even their livestock. Nevertheless, he "spared, Agag [the Amalekites' king], and the best of the sheep, and of the oxen, and of the fatlings, and the lambs, and all that was good, and would not utterly destroy them" (verse 9).

Then, to make matters worse, when the prophet Samuel arrived, Saul put on a false front of piety. Trying to sound very religious and claiming loyalty to the Lord, Saul greeted Samuel with the words: "Blessed be thou of the Lord: I have performed the commandment of the

Lord" (verse 13).

But Samuel wasn't fooled. He could hear the bleating and lowing of sheep and oxen that were supposed to be dead. So he flung a convicting question at Saul: "Hath the Lord as great delight in burnt offerings and sacrifices, as in obeying the voice of the Lord?" (verse 22). "Behold," Samuel continued, answering his own question, "to obey is better than sacrifice, and to hearken than the fat of rams." Finally, the prophet announced the Lord's sentence upon guilty Saul: "Because thou hast rejected the word of the Lord, he hath also rejected thee from being king" (verse 23).

The principle is clearly visible in this unfortunate situation, isn't it? Obeying the Lord's commandments is basic to pleasing the Lord. He would rather not have our busy service if He doesn't have our unqualified love which expresses itself in obedience to His Word.

Being sensitive to God's will is a greater asset than either academic brilliance or eloquence. There certainly was nothing of the scholar or orator in Edward Kimball. As a matter of fact, this humble Sunday School teacher was a rather timid man whose words didn't always come out just the way he wanted. But Edward Kimball believed in practicing what he taught, including soul winning. So he went into a shoe store one day in order to talk to one of his Sunday School students about salvation. What his faltering words lacked that day his compassion more than compensated for as he put his arm around the young shoe clerk and urged him to believe on the Saviour. The shoe clerk, who was converted to Christ then, was Dwight L. Moody. Moody became a mighty preacher of the gospel, whose evangelistic ministry influenced thousands on both sides of the Atlantic to turn to Jesus Christ.

There may not be another Dwight L. Moody waiting for your outreach, but perhaps your response to the mandate to "go" as well as to "stand and speak in the temple" will result in some unsaved person in your class coming into newness of life in Christ. And what a chain reaction that could set off!

A PREPARED HEART TO TEACH GOD'S WORD

We learn from Ezra 7:10 that Ezra prepared his heart not only to "seek the law of the Lord, and to do it," but also "teach in Israel statutes and judgments." I find the order in this to be extremely interesting and significant. Teaching followed seeking and doing.

That may seem like too slow a procedure for many in our hurry-up-and-assume-command society, but it is an essential procedure for those who want eternity to pervade their ministry. If a teacher wishes to point others in the right direction, he should be heading in that direction himself. If he expects others to run the Christian race well, he must be running well himself. No one should be expected to get very enthusiastic about listening to a Sunday School teacher describe the fruit of the Spirit unless samples of that fruit are on display in the teacher's life.

First things first, then. Serving as a Sunday School teacher is a high privilege, but the responsibilities are equally high. Prepare your heart to seek God's Word and to do it. Then, when you teach adults, they will recognize in you an effective model of the Christlike life.

QUICK REVIEW

1. A teacher's greatest asset is a head full of Bible facts.   T F

2. Ezra prepared his heart to seek God's law, to do it, and to teach it.   T F

14

3. Sunday School teaching doesn't require much time.   T   F

4. Understanding the context is essential to good Bible study.   T   F

5. A teacher should serve as an effective model of the Christlike life.   T   F

Answers:
1. F 2. T 3. F 4. T 5. T

2 What Good Teachers Are Made Of

Teachers come in assorted shapes and sizes. Some are short; some are tall. There are thin teachers and stout teachers. Some teachers are old, while others are young. Occasionally, you can find a teacher who looks like a pro athlete, but more often teachers look like average people in neat but unassuming attire. But all good teachers have something in common — a desire to communicate Jesus Christ by example as well as talk. This is why it is so important for a teacher to understand that we communicate by what we are as well as by what we say. To a certain extent, then, we may conclude that the teacher is not only the messenger but also the message.

Obviously, the good news about salvation and God's provision of peace and joy for those who belong to Him will be received more enthusiastically by students if their teacher's life gives evidence of transformation and contentment. It should prove helpful, then, to be aware of the major characteristics which present such evidence. First of all, a teacher must have experienced . . .

THE NEW BIRTH

Where would you begin if you launched into the

construction of a house? You would begin with the foundation, wouldn't you? After all, the stability of any house depends upon the foundation. Remember what the Lord Jesus taught about a house built on sand and another built on rock? The house on the sand buckled and collapsed under the impact of raging flood water, but the house on the rock endured the flood without damage. The principle of building on a solid foundation applies just as well to teaching the Bible. Unless a teacher has been born again, he can't expect to build a teaching ministry that will amount to anything worthwhile.

John, chapter 3, introduces us to a religious teacher who wasn't born again. His name was Nicodemus, and he was a Pharisee, a ruler of the Jews, and a teacher of Israel. No question about it, he carried clout as far as the Jews were concerned. He was loaded with credentials and stuffed to the phylacteries with religious learning. But, as far as God was concerned, Nicodemus lacked something that no amount of credentials and religious training could make up for. That something was the new birth. So Jesus told him forthrightly, "Ye must be born again" (verse 7). And what Nicodemus needed above everything else is precisely what every teacher must have, for being born again is foundational to Christian growth and service.

From the very moment that the new birth occurs, the Holy Spirit takes up permanent residence in the believer and, among other things, begins to help him understand the Scriptures. Jesus promised concerning this special ministry, "When he, the Spirit of truth, is come, he will guide you into all truth" (John 16:13). A teacher who hasn't been born again lacks this benefit and therefore cannot properly understand the Scriptures.

The Apostle Paul put it this way in I Corinthians 2:14: "But the natural man receiveth not the things of the Spirit of God: for they are foolishness unto him: neither can he know them, because they are spiritually discerned." It would be as impossible for an unregenerate teacher to communicate God's Word as it is for a blind-from-birth man to describe the radiant hues of a dazzling sunset falling on a tropical lagoon.

THE GIFT OF TEACHING

A good teacher is gifted. I don't mean to suggest that his I.Q. is in the genius range. Nor am I suggesting that a good teacher has the gift of being able to magnetize an audience so that they will cling to his every word. If our Sunday Schools depended upon such persons for the ministry of Christian education, we would be in dreadful shape, saddled with the greatest teacher shortage of all time. I simply mean a teacher ought to possess the gift of teaching — a spiritual gift — in order to serve effectively.

Paul refers to teaching as a spiritual gift in several passages of Scripture. In I Corinthians 12:4,28 he states: "Now there are diversities of gifts, but the same Spirit... And God hath set some in the church, first apostles, secondarily prophets, thirdly teachers . . . ." Writing to the believers at Rome, he explains: "Having then gifts differing according to the grace that is given to us, whether prophecy, let us prophesy according to the proportion of faith; Or ministry, let us wait on our ministering: or he that teacheth, on teaching" (Romans 12: 6,7). And, in Ephesians 4:11, he informs us that the risen Head of the church, the Lord Jesus Christ, "gave some, apostles; and some, prophets; and some, evangelists; and some, pastors and teachers." It is clear from these passages that God equips some in the church for the ministry of teaching. Those who have the gift of teaching should thank God for it, develop it, and use it wisely.

Naturally, a person may ask, "How can I know if I

have this gift? Should I expect to see the command, 'Teach,' written in the clouds? Should I anticipate a dream in which I see myself standing before a group of adults with a Bible in my right hand and a teacher's manual in my left hand?" The answer is no. While no two teachers enter into their responsibilities in precisely the same way, it seems that a pattern develops in bringing most teachers to the conviction that they have received the gift of teaching. There are four basic stages in this pattern, as follows.

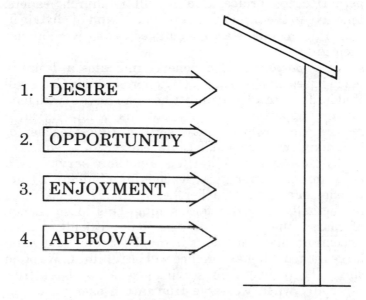

1. DESIRE

2. OPPORTUNITY

3. ENJOYMENT

4. APPROVAL

Indicators of the Spiritual Gift of Teaching

1) *Desire.* It is reasonable to suppose that God kindles a desire to teach in the heart of the one whom He has gifted for the ministry of teaching. Just as Paul, who was

divinely equipped to serve as an apostle, could not picture himself being happy unless he preached the gospel (see I Corinthians 9:16), even so anyone divinely equipped to teach God's Word will find himself longing for the opportunity to use his spiritual gift. In far too many churches, however, classes have teachers who are there because their arm was twisted rather than their heart inclined toward the teaching task.

Undoubtedly, in every church God has gifted a sufficient number of believers for the educational ministry of the church. The desire to teach should be permitted to surface, and it will if church leaders, sensitive to the will of God, create the kind of climate in which the members are encouraged to discover and use their gifts.

2) *Opportunity.* If a believer indicates a desire to teach based on a personal conviction that it is God's will that he do so, in all probability he won't have to wait long for the opportunity to try out his wings. I would recommend, however, that he serve as a guest teacher for a Sunday or act as a substitute teacher for a while.

3) *Enjoyment.* Whether a person serves as a substitute teacher, a guest teacher for a Sunday, a team teacher, or a regular teacher, he will enjoy the task if God has actually gifted him for teaching. This doesn't mean, of course, that there won't be some difficult — even uncomfortable — moments in the classroom, but by and large the teaching experience will be fulfilling. We often sing, "There is joy in serving Jesus"; and it's true, especially when we serve Him in the exercise of our spiritual gifts.

It isn't surprising, is it, to expect real enjoyment when we do what God has given us the ability to do? After all, in ordinary matters, people generally enjoy doing what they have the ability to do well. For example, a man with woodworking skills who holds down a five-days-a-week office job might have a hard time waiting for Saturday to arrive, the day when he can don an old pair of coveralls and saw, chip, chisel, plane, hammer, sand and varnish wood to his heart's content. Why, then, should we not expect someone with the spiritual gift of teaching to look forward eagerly to each Sunday's opportunity to enjoy teaching adults to his heart's content?

4) *Approval.* A person with the gift of teaching will meet with a measure of approval. Students will encourage him by remarking that they have been blessed by his teaching. Or, at least they will look interested during class and participate actively in the learning process. I doubt seriously that a person has the gift of teaching if his class sessions seem to drag, stall, crawl, and fizzle out like a defective Roman candle on the Fourth of July, leaving everyone disappointed and bewildered.

I have visited numerous adult classes, and have observed teachers create a learning situation that makes students want to come back for more. There was never any doubt in my thinking that these teachers were exercising the spiritual gift of teaching. But in other situations there was no doubt in my mind that the teachers were misplaced, for they obviously lacked that spiritual gift. Their students rarely looked at them, choosing rather to stare blankly at the floor, read a take-home paper, count the railings in the choir loft, and shake their wristwatches as if to speed up the remaining class time. Teachers in those situations should have been aware of a lack of approval upon their teaching and concluded that either they lacked the gift of teaching or had failed utterly to develop it. I suspect that some honest reflection on their part would have led them to the former conclusion.

If this frank discussion seems too harsh, let's remember that God's work deserves our best; and our best is only as good as the faithful exercise of our spiritual gifts. A person who has the proper attitude toward serving the Lord will not want to continue in the teaching office if he lacks the teaching gift. Rather, he will seek some other ministry which complements the gift(s) he does have. Surely, if all church members would function in the specific areas in which their spiritual gifts lie, there would be an adequate supply of Sunday School teachers and all the other service responsibilities would be filled too. And the results would be an effective church fellowship and powerful outreach for Christ.

A good teacher, then, is one who is born again and spiritually gifted for the ministry of teaching. But these alone are not sufficient. A teacher must also have ...

DEDICATION

Sometimes a person finds himself in the position of adult Sunday School teacher because the "local recruiter" broke down his resistance. Maybe the *coup de grace* was delivered by the recruiter when he lamented, "Won't you please take over the class? I can't think of anyone else to ask. It really won't demand much of your time." It isn't long, however, before the draftee finds out that teaching adults is far from an easy responsibility. He realizes soon enough that it takes time — lots of time — to prepare lessons and to carry on a helpful ministry in which students advance spiritually. He catches on to the fact that if he is going to hang in there week after week, month after month, even year after year, it's going to take a special quality. It's going to take *dedication*.

The Apostle Paul provides an excellent example for us to follow regarding dedication to the Lord and to the ministry of His Word. For instance, Paul stirred up a lot of disfavor among the opponents to the gospel in Ephesus when he preached Christ and organized a church. Frenzy broke out in Ephesus, and Paul's life was clearly in jeopardy. A lesser man than Paul might have packed his bags in a hurry and sneaked out of town under the cover of darkness. But dedication kept the apostle in Ephesus for as long as God had work for him to do there.

So, for three and a half years, he stayed in Ephesus, teaching the Word faithfully in spite of relentless opposition. When departure day arrived, he summoned the elders of the Ephesian church to meet with him and then he delivered his farewell address. Listen closely to a part of that address and catch the spirit of dedication from so great a man of God:

> ". . . I have been with you at all seasons, Serving the Lord with all humility of mind, and with many tears, and temptations, which befell me by the lying in wait of the Jews: And how I kept back nothing that was profitable unto you, but have shewed you, and have taught you publickly, and from house to house . . . neither count I my life dear unto myself, so that I might finish my course with joy, and the ministry, which I have received of the Lord Jesus, to testify the gospel of the grace of God" (Acts 20:18-20, 24).

Years later, with conditions still severe, Paul was maintaining that same degree of dedication. The executioner's sword was about to swoop down on Paul's neck. Undaunted, the apostle explained in II Timothy 4:6-8:

> "I am ready to be offered, and the time of my departure is at hand. I have fought a good fight, I have finished my course, I

> have kept the faith; Henceforth there is
> laid up for me a crown of righteousness,
> which the Lord, the righteous judge, shall
> give me at that day . . . ."

A life of dedication, that's what set Paul apart as a model
for all the followers of Christ through the centuries.
Teachers of God's Word who maintain a similar
dedication can surmount whatever obstacles they
encounter, and, like Paul, at life's end they can look
forward to the crown which the Master Teacher will give
to them.

BASIC KNOWLEDGE

A good teacher doesn't have to be a walking
encyclopedia, able to dispense right answers to all the
questions students raise. Nor does he need a college and
seminary education, although such training is certainly
excellent. But he does need a basic, working knowledge
in three areas: 1) his subject, 2) his students, and 3) how
to communicate effectively.

A teacher who doesn't know his subject will likely
fail to inspire confidence. His students will pity him
rather than accept his leadership. After all, who wants to
listen to someone who has practically nothing to say?
And who wants to follow someone who doesn't know
where he is going? Also, unless a teacher knows his
students — their level of understanding, their concerns,
interests, abilities, needs, and how they learn best — he
might as well teach a brick wall.

Finally, it is essential that a teacher know how to
communicate effectively. He must know when to speak,
what to say, and how to say it. He must also know when
to listen and how to listen. But a later chapter will deal
more thoroughly with these matters.

CHRISTIAN LOVE

"Though I speak with the tongues of men and of angels, and have not charity [love], I am become as sounding brass, or a tinkling cymbal" (I Corinthians 13:1). These words, written by the Apostle Paul, stress just how important a loving attitude is. Eloquence and clever public speaking are no substitute for it. Love in a teacher's heart is that indispensable quality that serves as an effective language in its own right, persuading students of the authenticity and practicality of Christianity.

Undoubtedly, many adults attend Sunday School regularly because some rather average teachers, in terms of teaching skills, manifest an above average ability to demonstrate supernatural love. Such teachers show that they love God and His Word by walking in the Truth, and they display a love for their students and their students' families by *being there* — to encourage, to counsel, to pray, to share in happy times and hard times.

By his own admission, Doug wasn't an outstanding Bible teacher. He was just average. But he demonstrated Christian love and, as a result, his adult Sunday School class was alive and well. Students were permitted ample opportunity each Sunday to share their burdens with one another, openly and honestly. Then the class engaged in specific, urgent prayer for one another's needs. During the week Doug led the way for others in the class to follow up the expressed concerns by telephoning and visiting to see what further help the class might offer. Such love in action created a classroom climate that was ideal for growth in Bible knowledge and life application.

Set in contrast to Doug's *modus operandi* the unfortunate situation in which a teacher with tons of Bible facts failed to show Christian concern for his students. Every Sunday he stood behind a homemade pulpit and expounded Scripture in routine lecture style until the final bell rang, announcing the end of the class session. A hurried-up prayer that the Lord "would seal to every heart the precious truths of the lesson" sent the adults scurrying off to the church auditorium for the morning service. Students' trials and deep-seated questioning about why no one seemed to care went unannounced, unnoticed, and unresolved. In time, class attendance plummeted to an all-time low, while the teacher tried to figure out how such a disaster could strike so knowledgeable a teacher as himself. His sad situation brings to mind Paul's warning: "And though I . . . understand all mysteries, and all knowledge . . . and have not charity [love], I am nothing" (I Corinthians 13:2).

A good teacher possesses more than one admirable quality, but none more important than Christian love.

PATIENCE

Students are individuals. Some have been Christians for a long time, some for a relatively short time. A few haven't yet trusted in the Saviour. So there are different levels of spiritual attainment represented by members of an adult Sunday School class. Not everyone in the class, therefore, will agree immediately with their teacher's views. Some may want to question. And some may voice their disagreements rather forcefully. Rather than losing his composure, a good teacher will exercise patience, gently responding to each student with Scriptural direction and dependence upon the Holy Spirit's ability to nurture students and teacher alike in a clearer understanding of the will of God. At all costs a teacher must not ridicule a student or shut him up in a high-handed manner.

A SENSE OF HUMOR

No one in his right mind would suggest that a teacher of adults must have a gag a minute up his sleeve. As a matter of fact, Bible teaching is too serious a responsibility to be handled in a comical manner. But those who have been blessed with a keen sense of humor know that it can be a very present help in time of trouble. It can be used as a tool to pry oneself and others, too, out of some embarrassing situations.

Take, for example, the case of the teacher who requested, "Now, let's have prayer, with every head closed and every eye bowed." His willingness to chuckle with the class later over his slip of the tongue helped the class relate better to him as a fallible, likable, *human* person. The same rapport was established in a class when the teacher, meaning to pray for people in rest homes, inadvertently asked for blessing upon "all our friends confined to rest rooms."

And, as everyone knows, an occasional humorous anecdote, used skillfully to illustrate a point, can spark the class's attention and help them remember an important spiritual principle.

So, teacher, learn to enjoy humor and know when and how to make it work for your students' good, recognizing that "a merry heart doeth good like a medicine" (Proverbs 17:22).

Obviously, the qualities found in good teachers exceed the list provided in this chapter, but these form a solid basis for influencing men and women to love the Word of God and the God of the Word. Each teacher can afford to bring his individual personality to the teaching process and trust God to refine his best qualities and employ them to His glory.

QUICK REVIEW

1. To a certain extent, the teacher is the message as well as the messenger.   T   F

2. The new birth is foundational to understanding the Scriptures.   T   F

3. Teaching is a spiritual gift.   T   F

4. If a person has the gift of teaching he will likely have a desire to teach.   T   F

5. Before a person becomes a regular teacher he should have a few trial teaching sessions.   T   F

6. Some approval of a person's teaching can be expected if he has the gift of teaching.   T   F

7. A teacher needs to have a basic knowledge of his subject, his students, and how to communicate effectively. T   F

8. The most admirable quality a teacher may possess is Christian love.   T   F

9. Under some circumstances it is all right for a teacher to ridicule a student.   T   F

10. Humor is out of place in an adult Sunday School class.   T   F

Answers:
1.T 2.T 3.T 4.T 5.T 6.T 7.T 8.T 9.F 10.F

3 Adults:
A Special Challenge

If you enjoy challenges, you ought to love teaching adults. Although Sunday School teachers at all grade levels face many challenges, it may be argued that those who teach adults encounter the greatest. The vast diversities characterizing adults provide one reason for this claim. The potential adults have for performing and financing Christian service is another. Still another is the proximity of adults to eternity in the normal course of living and dying. Adults as a whole do not have as much time left as others for doing the things that will gain the Master's approval at His judgment seat (I Corinthians 3:9-15; II Corinthians 5:9,10). The teacher of adults, then, must give himself to his task with a sense of urgency about effecting Christ-honoring changes in his students' lives.

WIDE-RANGING DIVERSITY

Standing before a class of adults in a church that has only one adult class (and I suspect this is more common than uncommon to the total ecclesiastical panorama), a teacher quickly recognizes that there is a great diversity of ages among the students. From about twenty years old to ninety years old, the adults attend Sunday School, hoping to derive from God's Word something significant for their Christian walk. Reaching out to the twenty-year-olds and to the ninety-year-olds, while touching the lives of everyone else in the class, presents a formidable challenge to the teacher.

But the challenge extends beyond age differences. Adults have educational differences too. The third grade teacher may have bright third-graders and below average third-graders in the same class, but she does have only third-graders in her class. The educational span in her class is not terribly wide. In the adult class, however, there may be high school dropouts, some who never started high school, college students, high school grads who didn't go on to college, college grads, and even one or two persons with doctorates. Such an educational mix finds the teacher wondering how to approach the class. Should he try to establish a highly academic atmosphere in order to appeal to the students with the advanced educational training? Should he scale down the lesson content in order to appeal to those with limited educational training? While there isn't an easy answer to the teacher's dilemma, I would like to point out a couple of important factors for consideration.

Factor One. Intelligence is a very complex quality, hard to define and often misunderstood. Who is to say whether a person with a minimal education is less intelligent than a person with a great deal of education? What he lacks in formal learning may be more than compensated for by an obvious possession of common sense.

One person may have lots of factual knowledge. Another may have uncanny social knowledge, being able to win and keep a great many friends of different personality types. Another person's intelligence may show up in his ability to succeed in business even though he didn't study economics and business management in school. Still another person with minimal education may be an expert mechanic or construction worker, the envy of at least one PhD who hasn't learned to change the oil in his car or build a doghouse for Rover.

So a wise teacher will avoid the notion that some in the class are intelligent and others are not intelligent. He will respect every person and recognize that he has something worthwhile to contribute to the class.

A further word of caution is in order at this point. Although a good education brings a certain advantage for learning the Scriptures, it is not the critical criterion for determining who can be a knowledgeable Bible student. The Holy Spirit can lead any Christian into a deep and highly practical knowledge of the Word. The key factors are a willing heart, a diligent spirit, and a love for the God of the Word and the Word of God.

I can think of an adult class — a rather large class — in which quite a few college graduates are enrolled along with a variety of other adults, including Wilbur. Most persons who know Wilbur would tell you that he is somewhat retarded. But they would also tell you that he is one of the sharpest Bible students in that adult class. In succession, several Bible college professors have taught the class and each admits to having been put on the hot spot at one time or another by an insightful Bible question from Wilbur. They would tell you that the Holy Spirit performs a remarkable teaching ministry to anyone, regardless of educational training, whose heart is right before God and desirous of His instruction.

Factor Two. Vocabulary doesn't have to be profound to convey profound truth. Don't burn the midnight oil studying a dictionary in search for big and unusual words that might impress the highly educated class members. When you teach in class, speak conversationally. Use the vocabulary range that you use Monday through Saturday. Ordinary words can have extraordinary effectiveness when they are employed in the power of the Holy Spirit. Remember what the Apostle Paul told the Corinthians? "And I, brethren, when I came to you, came not with excellency of speech or of wisdom, declaring unto you the testimony of God. And my speech and my preaching was not with enticing words of man's wisdom, but in demonstration of the Spirit and of power" (I Corinthians 2:1,4). And recall how the Lord Jesus Christ communicated. He employed simple, often one-syllable words, when He taught. And it didn't matter whether He was addressing the learned or the rank and file of the population. He didn't use $64,000 words in His famous Sermon on the Mount or in any of His parables, yet there was more than enough depth in what He said to challenge the thinking of philosophers and theologians from the first century until now. And "the common people heard him gladly" (Mark 12:37).

So a wise teacher won't break his pedagogical back by leaning too far in the direction of the highly educated or in the direction of the least well-educated. He will just be himself and use the vocabulary and style with which he is most comfortable.

It is likely, however, that as a teacher of adults you will find the better educated students more open and spontaneous about voicing an opinion, fielding a question, raising an issue, and sharing their views and experiences. If you provide the right climate for such students to do these sorts of things, you will keep them happy and sustain their interest week after week. At the same time, you will be providing the less confident class members a good model for involvement.

Another way to keep outgoing, more highly educated persons interested in the class sessions is to give them outside work — research, opinion gathering, commentary reports, and other assignments. During class sessions they could serve as discussion leaders, buzz group captains, or debate team members, etc.

If you do find that the educational diversity becomes

a problem and your best efforts to solve it fail, perhaps you should speak to your superintendent, director of Christian Education, the chairman of the Christian Education Committee, or the pastor. An electives system may be devised that would group the adults according to their specific interests and abilities and thereby solve your problem while breathing new life into the adult department of the Sunday School.

A second challenge related to teaching adults concerns the wide-ranging levels of Christian growth. Sometimes an adult class consists of persons just recently saved, others well-advanced in the number of years saved, and the rest somewhere between the two extremes. While we might assume that the longer a person has been a Christian the more mature he is as a believer, this may not be the case.

It is quite possible that a Christian of many years standing has coasted along without applying himself diligently to the study of Scripture and its application to his life. On the other hand, a fairly recent convert may be advancing in the knowledge of God and His Word at a rapid pace because of his devotion to personal Bible study.

So, for one reason or another, the teacher of adults faces a heterogeneous group in terms of their Christian growth differences. What is he to do? That's the challenge.

If I may coin a term, this is where *motivational mix* comes into play. By motivational mix I mean the stimulation to learn and to grow which adults at each level of Christian development derive from those at the other levels. For example, new Christians can learn important Bible truths from older Christians whose knowledge of the Scriptures is keen. They can learn from them, too, what to expect in the Christian life — how to establish and maintain a quiet time, how to witness, how to cope with trials, how to resist temptations, and a host of other things. In turn, Christians who have been along the pilgrim road for quite some time can profit from the new converts' joyful exuberance and zeal to tell others about Christ. Sunday School, then, can become an enthusiastic time of interaction, sharing of Scripture, and interchanging of helpful experiences and ideas.

But one thing can stifle all of this faster than anything else. Straight lecture! If the teacher talks all the time, every Sunday, his students will not have the opportunity to interact. Motivational mix, then, will be a lost cause.

Diversity among adults in Sunday School also encompasses social and economic differences. Adults come from various social and economic backgrounds. Some are strapped with excessively high house payments, while others have their homes nearly paid for. A few may have practically no financial burdens. Some men and women in the class may be struggling with feelings of boredom and self-worthlessness, while others are facing new challenges and feel they are contributing a great deal at home and at work. Some adults feel lonely. Others, caught up in a whirlwind of social activity, may be longing for a quieter, more relaxed life-style.

Some have grown up in secure families, while others have had to cope with the anguish caused by a broken home. There may be divorcees in the class, along with married couples reaching for their 25th, 40th, or 50th wedding anniversary. Engaged couples and single-for-life men and women may be members of the same class. Some students may have a wide circle of non-Christian friends. Others may have practically no non-Christian friends.

The class may include an executive with ulcers, a mother who can't handle her teenage daughter, a terminally ill cancer victim, an ambitious business entrepreneur, an unemployed factory worker, and a variety of other adults, all of them with very different needs.

Still another kind of diversity among adults stems from their wide-ranging interests. From crocheting to sky-diving, from reading to remodeling, from fishing to flying, their interests are many and dissimilar. Naturally, a teacher can't be expected to be knowledgeable in every interest area, but having an awareness of just how wide-ranging the class interests are will help a teacher to recognize the challenge facing him. And, of course, knowing what the students' interests are will help a teacher to choose illustrations that will appeal to the class.

It's a fact that whenever a teacher focuses on an area of student interest class attention rises to a higher level. Isn't this evident in our Saviour's teaching? He illustrated spiritual truth by referring to things which lay within the range of His audiences' interests. The weather. Taxes. Food, clothing, shelter. Friendship. Farming. Fishing. Family. Sheep and shepherding. Eating, drinking, and working. No wonder no one was neutral to what Jesus had to say!

So there's a lot of diversity among adults, which presents some problems. But the challenge of it all can make teaching adults exciting and one of the most satisfying ministries in the church.

POTENTIAL: WAKE IT UP

A discouraged pastor once observed, "My church is full of willing workers: some are willing to work, and the rest are willing to let them." Wouldn't it be great if your church had enough workers for all the tasks needing to be accomplished? This is where teaching adults becomes the recruiting and training arm of the church. Your class can become the seedbed from which fruitbearing

Christians spring up.

How will this happen? Through your faithful sharing of the Scriptures with your students. The Bible implanted in their innermost being will create an itch to do God's will. "How can I contribute to the ministry of my church?" "Isn't there some job in the church I can perform?" "When can I start developing my spiritual gifts in serving the Lord?" These are the kinds of questions maturing members of your class will ask.

So, don't be surprised when names start disappearing from your class roll because men and women leave your class in order to assume service roles in the Sunday School. And don't be surprised several weeks before the church's annual meeting to find several class members listed on the slate of nominees for church officers. Consider all of this firm evidence that spiritual growth has been occurring in your class, and accept the continuing challenge to launch even more of your students into active Christian service in your Sunday School and church.

Something else to think about in terms of the challenge teaching adults presents — most of the burden of financial support for your church and its missionary program falls squarely on the shoulders of its adult membership. If men and women fail to give liberally according to the manner in which God has prospered them, the church will not be able to add new missionaries to its support list. But, as they mature in their knowledge of the Bible, they will become increasingly aware of the heartbeat of God for missions, and they will catch the spirit of missions in such a way that they will give generously and prayerfully to the cause of missions.

PROXIMITY TO ETERNITY:
A SERIOUS CHALLENGE

I recall an elderly deacon in a testimonial service exhorting himself and the rest of the members of the church to buy up the moments in service for Christ. He put it this way: "None of us knows how much longer we have for serving the Lord on this earth. Soon the old *must* leave, and at any moment the young *may* leave."

He was right, of course, and while his exhortation carries a challenge to the young as well as the old, it most certainly packs a wallop for adults, particularly older adults. In the normal life span adults are left with fewer years than the young for serving Christ. Eternity is close to adults, which brings accounting day so close.

As a teacher of adults, you can perform an important service by guiding your students into a closer walk with the Lord and the daily experience of doing His will. Someday, when you stand with them at Christ's judgment seat, you will be overjoyed that you accepted the challenge of teaching the class. And so will they!

QUICK REVIEW

1. It isn't difficult to teach adults of wide-ranging ages in the same class.   T   F

2. One difficulty in teaching adults arises from their diverse educational backgrounds.   T   F

3. It is easy to measure intelligence.   T   F

4. There are different kinds of intelligence.   T   F

5. It is impossible to keep highly educated class members interested in a class that consists of many with less formal education.   T   F

6. The wide-ranging levels of Christian growth represented by adults presents a challenge to the teaching ministry.   T   F

7. This chapter coins the term "motivational mix" to mean the stimulation to learn and to grow which adults at each level of Christian development derive from those at the other levels. T F

8. Straight lecture can destroy motivational mix. T F

9. Student needs and interests should be given consideration in the teaching process. T F

10. An adult class should contribute a steady flow of workers to the ministries of the church. T F

4 Keeping Things in Balance

In Denver, Colorado, where I live, the favorite color is orange. No doubt about it, orange is everywhere except on Denver's paper money. Orange T-shirts, orange tennis shoes, orange hats, orange plates, orange coffee mugs, orange desk lamps, orange clocks, orange carnations, and *ad orange infinitum*. Why, you can even find orange pizza in Denver. It's all part of the "Orange Crush Mania" that first squeezed this city and region into the 1978 Super Bowl at the close of a sensational Denver Broncos football season.

Up until now, though, the Broncos — Denver's great orange hope — haven't delivered a Super Bowl victory, and many fans believe the reason has been the team's apparent lack of balance. Nearly everyone has heard about the "Orange Crush Defense" with its phenomenal ability to stop the opposing team cold and pull off "miracle" interceptions. But what about the Broncos' offense? Well, that's a different story! Suffice it to say, it takes a balance between good defense and good offense to provide a winning combination. So until that develops, Denverites will have to be content to live with orange dreams.

But balance isn't just important in football; it's also important in teaching adults in Sunday School. We might be able to work up some excitement without it, but in the end our teaching will fail to accomplish everything we had hoped for. I'm referring to the balance that ought to exist between Bible information (content, indoctrination) and life application. Both are as essential to a healthy spiritual life as diet and exercise are to a healthy physical life.

INFORMATION AND APPLICATION
IN THE OLD TESTAMENT

Throughout the Old Testament infallible data abounds. We learn truths about God, creation, the entrance of sin into the world, the conflict that exists between righteousness and unrighteousness, God's plan of redemption, His holy laws, and His assurances that blessing will rest upon those who love and obey Him while judgment rests upon those who despise His grace and renounce His will. But this teaching isn't confined to theological statements, commandments and statutes, although these abound in the Old Testament, particularly in the Pentateuch. A host of flesh and blood illustrations parade across the pages of the Old Testament to demonstrate that we cannot trifle with the information God gives in His Word. And another host of men and women march through the Old Testament to show us how satisfying and rewarding it is to respond by faith to God's declarations and commands.

We learn, for example, from God's prohibition to Adam in the garden in Eden just how important it is to God that we obey Him. By watching what happened to Adam when he rebelled against that prohibition we learn that sin doesn't pay. From Exodus through Deuteronomy we read God's commandments, statutes and judgments with accompanying promises and warnings. Then, alongside this information, God gives us the drama of Moses and Israel so that we might learn about Him through His dealings with faithful Moses and unfaithful Israel. But learning through real-life drama doesn't stop when we get to the end of Deuteronomy. Just think about all the spiritual truth we can gather from Joshua through Malachi by studying about God's dealings with Captain Joshua, Israel's judges, Saul, David, Solomon, the rest of the kings, and the prophets.

And who can't help but see a happy balance in Psalms and Proverbs between facts about God and personal relationships with Him? It's a balance that helps us in our quest to know Him better and to serve Him well.

Content and application, then, belong in our teaching. We cannot neglect either one without running counter to the way God teaches truth in the Old Testament. Perhaps Joshua 1:8 capsulizes for us the entire Old Testament's balanced perspective, for it brings together in one verse the perfect balance of content and application.

"This book of the law shall not depart out of thy mouth; but thou shalt meditate therein day and night . . . **Content**

"that thou mayest observe to do according to all that is written therein: for then thou shalt make thy way prosperous, and then thou shalt have good success." **Application**

INFORMATION AND APPLICATION
IN THE NEW TESTAMENT

When our Lord Jesus Christ lived among men He taught many wonderful truths and did many wonderful things. He brought God's message to man not only in word but also in deed. As a matter of fact He both spoke the truth and was the truth. He gave information about God and declared His will, but He also portrayed God by doing His will without deviating from it in the slightest way. Furthermore, our Lord made it plain that we are supposed to apply the truths He taught. He said, "If ye know these things, happy are ye if ye do them" (John 13:17). Again, we see the balance between information (content) and application.

In the book of Acts, too, we see this all-important balance between information and application. Much has been written and discussed concerning the enthusiastic and effective outreach of the early church. Its evangelistic history makes the book of Acts not only exciting reading but a textbook for finding out how the twentieth-century church can improve its outreach for Christ.

From a starting point in Jerusalem the church in Acts spread its Christian witness across Judea, penetrated into Samaria, carved its way through Asia Minor, and pushed on into Europe. Eventually, the whole Roman empire felt the impact of this missionary drive. In other ways, too, the church of Acts was an outstanding church. Its fellowship was unified, caring, worshipful and generous. But foundational to all of this was its devotion to learning doctrine. Acts 2:42 indicates that the believers in the primitive history of the church at Jerusalem "continued stedfastly in the apostles' doctrine."

Indoctrination (information, content), then, was the "stuff" from which fellowship, worship, and evangelism developed. The teaching ministry, therefore, must lay a solid foundation of Biblical content upon which appropriate relationships and witness may be established.

The New Testament epistles, too, depict a balance between information (content, indoctrination) and application. Paul's epistles in particular abound with both emphases, but Romans, Galatians and Ephesians are so clearly structured with application following indoctrination that no one should fail to see the balance.

ROMANS

Information (Doctrine)   *Application*
Chapters 1 — 11   Chapters 12 — 16

GALATIANS

Biography   *Information (Doctrine)*   *Application*
Chapters 1 — 2   Chapters 3 — 4   Chapters 5 — 6

EPHESIANS

Information (Doctrine)   *Application*
Chapters 1 — 3   Chapters 4 — 6

What is characteristic of Paul's epistles is also characteristic of James' epistle, the Epistle to the Hebrews, the Epistle of Jude, and John's epistles. Doctrine and duty — information and application — fit together like a hand and glove. Even the book of Revelation, John's last inspired New Testament book, establishes a balance between prophetic information and practical application. Chapters 2, 3 and 22 are particularly applicable to daily living, inspiring us to make every moment count for God in view of Christ's imminent return.

So those who wish to de-emphasize Bible content and concentrate all of their attention upon relational situations are not following the Biblical format. By the same token, those who emphasize Bible content to the neglect of practical application are just as guilty of ignoring the Biblical format.

CURRENT TRENDS
AND APPEAL FOR CAUTION

Having thought about the balance in Scripture between information and application we are better able to evaluate some of the trends in Christian education that a teacher of adults needs to be aware of.

Behavioral Objectives

There is certainly nothing wrong with wanting to see effective change taking place among Christian adults. Every teacher of adults should pray for his students to this end. They need to be progressing in the Christian life by not only knowing the Bible better but also doing and being what it counsels. However, there is a pressing danger that a teacher might expect every student to respond to a lesson in precisely the same way. And there is also the unfortunate possibility that a teacher will feel that a lesson is not worth teaching unless it states a specific behavioral objective for the students.

Those who advocate having specific behavioral objectives for every lesson usually argue that our Sunday Schools are full of people with heads loaded with Bible information (content). These Christians need to know how to apply what they know, according to the argument. Therefore, teachers ought to be challenging their students to do specific things in response to the Word of God. But we may ask these advocates a few questions.

1) *Do Christians really have a very extensive knowledge of the Bible?* I think not! Although I would not wager my eternal security on it, I believe only a minority of adults in our churches have an abundant knowledge of God's Word. In my judgment, topical preaching from too many pulpits and sketchy Bible coverage in too many Sunday Schools along with very little personal Bible study on the part of rush-about

Christians has produced scores of Bible illiterates in our churches. If Christians are not behaving like mature Christians, the fault probably doesn't lie with too much Bible knowledge but with too little.

2) *Who can say what specific behavioral objective on a given Sunday is right for everyone in an adult class?* Adults cannot be pigeonholed. Life is far too complex for seeing every person at a certain point in the Christian life and requiring advancement to another point predetermined by the teacher or the curriculum specialist. The fact is, the specific behavioral objective that is selected on a given Sunday may have been reached by some class members five weeks ago or five years ago and may be inappropriate for others who are endeavoring to attain some different but equally important objectives.

It is interesting that some Christian education "specialists" seem to feel that a specific behavioral objective can be set for each student in every Sunday School lesson when Christian counselors often find it necessary to meet with a client for several sessions before agreeing upon an appropriate behavioral objective. Most counselors are keenly aware of how unique each person is and how much time it takes to help a client see what his real problem is and what goals he should claim in the process of changing his behavior.

3) *Shall we not teach passages of Scripture that are not behavior oriented?* Undoubtedly there are many chapters in God's Word that are not slanted primarily toward effecting behavioral change. Some of these relate to God's acts in history, and some describe God's sovereignty and glory. In response to these passages of Scripture we can appreciate God for who He is and contemplate His majesty — without setting any specific behavioral goal. Nevertheless, the learning that takes place can please God and deepen our spirituality. In time — but not necessarily within a week or in a specific behavioral task — our enriched sense of God's person and

work will shape our lives according to His will.

I have raised these questions simply out of a desire to urge caution in the use of behavioral objectives. A human being, having been created by God Himself, is far too complex to be treated like a machine. We cannot simply arrange the gears a certain way and set up a circuit so that a person will perform a prescribed task at the flick of a switch. While every Christian ought to apply God's Word in ways that will affect his behavior for his own good and God's glory, his teacher ought to respect his individuality and not force him into a behavioral shoe that doesn't fit.

Needs

No one will deny the fact that every human being has needs. It is rather basic to mankind to need not only food, clothing, and shelter — basic survival needs — but also a sense of well-being, acceptance, forgiveness, love, security and personal growth. Through the exercise of abundant divine grace God promises to meet these needs. Matthew 6:33 encourages us to trust God to provide the necessities of life, and other passages of Scripture give us assurance that in Christ we have acceptance, forgiveness, security and love. The Bible also teaches us how to enjoy a sense of well-being, or inner peace, and how to achieve fulfillment by doing God's will.

A teacher, then, has a marvelous opportunity to share these assurances with his students, but his desire to minister to their needs should not command his full attention. In other words, being aware of students' needs, as much as it is possible to know each student's needs, can help a teacher to personalize certain lesson truths, but he must not think a lesson lacks any value if it is not structured on needs.

As we have already considered in this book, adults are a highly diverse group of human beings. Their individual needs differ, so that on a given Sunday it would be impossible to gear a lesson to meeting certain specific needs and thereby include everyone's needs.

Furthermore, too much emphasis upon needs may lead some Christians to assume falsely that God's Word is only valuable if it satisfies their personal needs. This, of course, would be tantamount to taking a low view of Scripture by which it is evaluated by subjective reasoning and made subservient to human experience. A person may soon regard portions of Scripture as "good if they meet my needs, and not relevant if they don't meet my needs."

An overemphasis on needs borders on the promotion of a philosophy of "selfism," a concern for oneself as the ultimate reason for existing. It is a philosophy that runs counter to the Christian ethic that insists upon putting others' interests ahead of our own and ministering unselfishly to others (see Philippians 2:3,4; Mark 10:35-45). As I see it, teaching people to judge a lesson's worth on the basis of how well it meets their needs is flirting with this "selfism" philosophy.

In his book *Psychology as Religion* (Eerdmans, 1977, pp. 95, 96) Paul C. Vitz suggests, "Selfism is an example of a horizontal heresy, with its emphasis only on the present, and on self-centered ethics. At its very best (which is not often), it is Christianity without the first commandment." That commandment, of course, directs our attention away from ourselves as the object of our worship and toward God as the only One who deserves our worship. It is a commandment which should make us realize that God doesn't exist simply to serve our needs. He is the sovereign Creator who has a right to our love. A teacher, then, ought to stimulate his students to love God for who He is rather than thinking of Him as a kind of celestial Santa Claus who is important mainly because He can respond to whatever we have on our list of needs.

Again, balance is the key word. Adults have needs,

and a teacher ought to be sensitive to them and try to minister to them, but needs must not dominate his teaching.

Value Clarification

Christians ought to hold values that are truly worthwhile. And those values are apt to be quite different from the values held by unregenerated society. Doing God's will, for example, ought to be held as a higher value than accumulating material things, for I John 2:17 affirms that "the world passeth away, and the lust thereof: but he that doeth the will of God abideth for ever." But in the process of clarifying values God's Word must not be pushed aside so that students simply state what their values are and fail to expose them to the authority of Scripture.

Relational Learning

An emphasis exists today, and rightly so, on learning how to live the Christian life by seeing it demonstrated in appropriate relationships. Christians getting along in a mutually edifying and helpful way in a variety of relationships, including the church and the home, becomes an important factor in Christian education. But once again I raise the question, Is there not reason to be cautious in the adoption of this trend? There must not be an overemphasis on relationships to the neglect of Bible content. Both are important and should be held in balance.

Perhaps the most ardent advocate of relational learning is Larry Richards. But he is careful to push for balance between propositional truth — the Scriptures — and relationships that are exemplary. In his *A Theology of Christian Education* (Zondervan Publishing House, 1975, pp. 250, 251) he writes:

... For *all* ages the model is essential; a relationship with the model in which identification is encouraged and significant sharing of the inner life of teacher and learner takes place is critical; a "real life" rather than formal setting for shared experience is vital.

Please note that in defining these three dimensions of the teaching/learning process I am *not* "leaving out" the Word. The process defines *how* Scripture's "meaning for life" is shared: the fact that the Christian faith and life are essentially biblical is implicit. The correspondence between Scripture's portrait of the believer's faith and life, and the model's actual character and life style, is, of course, a keystone in true Christian education.

As a teacher of adults, help your students see the kinds of relationships they should emulate, but make certain that they let the Scriptures determine for them whether a relationship is worthy of their respect and copying.

Other trends in Christian education could be identified and discussed in this chapter, but enough have been singled out to underscore the importance of keeping things in balance. The Word of God is our sole authority for faith and practice, and a trend is only worthy of our acceptance if it furthers the effective entrance of God's Word into the inner life and public life of each student.

QUICK REVIEW

1. The Old Testament is only informational.   T   F

2. Paul's epistles are both theological and practical. T   F

3. Three of Paul's epistles that contain a doctrinal section before an application section are Romans, Galatians and Ephesians.   T   F

4. Joshua 1:8 capsulizes how information and application fit together.   T   F

5. It is very difficult to establish meaningful behavioral objectives in a given week for a whole class of adults. T   F

6. An overemphasis on needs can lead to selfism. T   F

7. In relational learning the Word of God must be the final judge of whether a relationship is right or wrong.   T   F

Answers:
1. F 2. T 3. T 4. T 5. T 6. T 7. T

5 Communication Bridges

Teaching adults demands more than a good Bible knowledge; it demands a working knowledge of communication. Knowing how to present God's message to students in such a way that they will receive it appropriately is an essential element in the communication process. In this chapter we shall think about some of the bridges which establish effective communication between teacher and students, but first we need to understand that communication involves a source, a message, a channel, and a receiver.

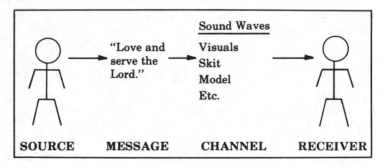

In the preceding diagram we can see a typical teacher-student communication setting, although it is hoped that in a Sunday School class communication would flow not only from teacher to student but also from student to teacher. The source is the teacher who sends a message through some channel or channels to a receiver (each student in the class). Obviously, each element in the communication process is critical to effective communication.

The teacher (source) must be an effective message sender. The message must be clear and accurate and hold relevant information. The channel must assist the source in delivering the message to the receiver. And the receiver (each student) must receive the message, interpret it correctly, internalize it, and respond appropriately to it. When all of these conditions are fulfilled, it is safe to say that effective communication has transpired.

Now, let's examine some communication bridges.

One of the most basic bridges for getting God's truth across to students in an effective manner is —

THE TEACHER AS AN APPROPRIATE MODEL

This has been alluded to earlier in this book, but it bears repeating; a teacher ought to be a living illustration of the truth he verbalizes. This was certainly true of the Apostle Paul. He advised the Philippian Christians: "Brethren, be followers together of me" (Philippians 3:17). His life and teaching complemented each other.

When Paul wrote to Timothy, a young pastor, he instructed him not only to *teach* "words of faith and of good doctrine" (compare I Timothy 4:6 and 11) but also to live in such a way that his attitudes and conduct would model the truth. "Be thou an example of the believers," Paul counseled, "in word, in conversation, in charity, in spirit, in faith, in purity" (verse 12).

In leading workshops, I have often asked those in attendance to write down what impressed them most about the best Sunday School teacher they ever had. Invariably, comments about a godly life comprised the number one response. I conclude, therefore, on the basis of personal experience and Scriptural emphasis, that a teacher who appropriately models God's truth is a bridge for effectively communicating this truth to students.

A COMMODIOUS CLASSROOM

Later in this book I'll be discussing classroom seating arrangement and the teaching/learning aids that should be available in a classroom, but at this point I want to stress how important other physical features are.

A classroom ought to be well ventilated, well lighted and kept at a comfortable temperature. A teacher may find it advantageous to give someone the responsibility of caring for these conditions so that, as much as possible, the students will feel comfortable and be able to see well. Each student should have enough elbow and leg room, too, for the sake of personal comfort. And the classroom decor should be attractive.

In *Approaching Speech/Communication* (Holt, Rinehart and Winston, Inc., 1974, p. 142) Michael Burgoon suggests: "Our environment both communicates and impinges upon the communication process. The way we design and use the elements in our environment transmits messages about ourselves." Every effort should be expended, then, to establish a classroom environment that communicates positive messages about the gospel and the rest of God's truth.

Also in his book (p. 142) Burgoon makes an interesting reference to the importance of an attractive environment in shaping attitudes. He writes:

> . . . In one study, subjects rated photographs of people's faces significantly higher in attractiveness when the subjects were in a "beautiful" room than when they were in an "ugly" room. Unattractive rooms are seen as fatiguing and displeasing, whereas attractive rooms tend to create feelings of well-being.

Perhaps Burgoon's conclusion may be carried over into the context of an adult Sunday School class. It may be equally the case that an attractive Sunday School classroom tends to elevate students' appreciation of the truths of Scripture.

CATCHING STUDENTS' INTEREST

It is questionable whether good communication can be established in a class session if a teacher fails to catch the students' interest. And certainly the time to catch that interest is at the beginning of the lesson presentation. A provocative question, a reference to some controversial issue, a humorous anecdote, a good illustration, a startling but brief statistical report, an update on an incident of great concern to the students — these are various ways of catching interest at the beginning of a class session. But it isn't sufficient to construct this bridge alone; other communication bridges are necessary as the lesson progresses.

EYE CONTACT

Still another bridge for effective communication is eye contact. Unless a teacher looks at his class he cannot expect to establish rapport with his students. In a later chapter, we shall think about how to prepare a lesson. If a teacher follows the ideas presented in that chapter, he will not be so bogged down in looking at his notes that he has little time for looking at his class. In using eye contact a teacher ought to look at the whole class, recognizing their presence and showing that he is interested in them. He ought to look directly at small groups in the class, giving his attention for a moment to one group, then to another, and so on. And he ought to look directly at individuals in the class. All of this holds the students' attention and gives the teacher important feedback. The expression on each face will tell whether a person is agreeing or disagreeing with what is being said. It will indicate whether he wants to ask a question or needs some time to think about a certain point. It will reveal whether what is being said is making an impact.

GOOD LISTENING

Since communication is a two-way street, a teacher needs to listen well to what his students have to say. And he needs to listen carefully — with his eyes as well as his ears — to how they are saying it! The *affect* associated with a person's statements often suggests whether or not he really believes what he is saying. For example, someone who rolls his eyes while alleging that rearing teenagers is an easy job is showing by his affective behavior that he really thinks it isn't such an easy job.

It is also important to effective communication that a teacher listen fully to what his students say. By doing so, he is showing them that he respects their individuality and worth. And as he listens, he learns what areas of interest and need demand further Biblical treatment.

CLEAR AND UNCLUTTERED SPEECH

A teacher can build a bridge for effective communication by speaking distinctly and loudly enough to be heard by everyone. But how well his students receive what he says also depends upon the clarity of his language. It should be free of mixed metaphors, vague abstractions and pious cliches. Terms should be carefully defined. Speaking should be fluent, spontaneous and natural. Pauses should come at the right places for effect. Enthusiasm and gestures should enhance a teacher's delivery. Variety in voice pitch can be the spice of speaking, and proper enunciation can keep students from whispering among themselves, "What did he just say?"

A VITAL CONCLUSION

Since teaching God's Word aims at bettering students in terms of their relationships with God and others, no one should walk away from Sunday School with the feeling that nothing was accomplished in the class session. Every lesson, then, ought to have a meaningful conclusion — something that helps every student see how the truth presented through the lesson and its accompanying activities ought to affect him. After all, in the communication of God's Word the message ought to be not only delivered appropriately but also received appropriately. So the teacher ought to help his students see how the truth applies to them. In the process of offering a good conclusion, though, the teacher should recognize that many different responses can be appropriate, depending upon each student's level of spirituality.

QUICK REVIEW

1. This chapter identifies a teacher as a source of communication. 					T F

2. It is accurate to say that a teacher may also be a channel of communication. 					T F

3. It appears that the attractiveness of a classroom helps to give students a higher concept of spiritual truth. 	T F

4. A teacher should avoid establishing eye contact with individuals in his class. 					T F

5. A conclusion to a lesson is effective only when every student responds to God's truth in an identical way. 	T F

Answers:
1. T 2. T 3. T 4. F 5. F

6 The Tools of the Trade

Anyone knows that it takes the right tools to do a job the right way. Nothing is quite so frustrating as trying to repair a leaky elbow joint under the kitchen sink with only a worn-out wrench and personal determination, or endeavoring to construct a treehouse for the kids with only a hammer, some nails, a pile of lumber and a tree. Well, teaching adults requires the right tools too — that is, if a teacher wants to do the best possible job. In this chapter we'll examine the kinds of tools that are available for teaching adults, considering first books, then curriculum materials, next audiovisuals, and finally a resource card file.

BOOKS

A visit to a Christian bookstore reveals that an overwhelming number of books are waiting to be purchased. Obviously, as much as a teacher might want to buy everything in the store, he may need to limit his buying to a few books at a time. Where will he begin to build his library?

A Bible. Sounds basic, doesn't it? And it is, for a

teacher's most important book is his Bible. But so many kinds of Bibles exist that a teacher must make a choice. Will he select a study Bible, complete with annotations, concordance, maps, topical index, and charts? Or will he opt for a Bible that has nothing but the text of Scripture? Will he go for one that has wide margins and small print, or will he prefer large print even though the margins are too narrow to accommodate his personal notes?

Although no one can say dogmatically what is best for every teacher, my personal preference dictates having two Bibles: a study Bible full of helps, which can be used for lesson preparation, and an uncluttered, easy-to-read Bible for teaching. However, if a teacher could purchase only one Bible, I would cast my vote for a study Bible. The *New Scofield Reference Bible, The Ryrie Study Bible,* or *Thompson's New Chain Reference Bible* would serve any teacher well.

Bible Atlas. This handy reference book contains maps of Bible lands, sometimes with interesting and informative comments. While the cost of a Bible atlas depends upon its complexity and size, its value to a teacher of adults is immeasurable. Using a Bible atlas, a teacher can become familiar with the geography that is so much a part of the Biblical record, and he can employ that familiarity to good advantage by giving his students a vivid awareness of the surroundings of Bible characters and events.

Suppose, for example, that a teacher calls the attention of his class to I Samuel 3:20 so that everyone may appreciate how widespread Samuel's reputation was as the Lord's prophet. The statement of I Samuel 3:20 is: "And all Israel from Dan even to Beersheba knew that Samuel was established to be a prophet of the Lord." Without the teacher's identification of Dan and Beersheba as towns, some in the class might assume they were a man and a woman and take a "So what?"

attitude. Others, knowing that they were towns but being unaware of their locations, might take a similar attitude.

But once the teacher, armed with information received from his Bible atlas, points out that Dan and Beersheba lay respectively at the northern and southern extremities of Israel, the students all gain a full appreciation of I Samuel 3:20's statement. They understand that the *whole* country recognized that God had given Israel a prophet.

There's no doubt about it, a Bible atlas will open up new vistas of Bible knowledge for a teacher and his students too.

Concordance. Like a Bible atlas, a concordance can be expensive or relatively inexpensive depending upon its size and contents. A teacher should examine concordances carefully and decide upon one that meets his needs best before making a purchase.

A concordance lists alphabetically the main words of the Bible, and serves several purposes.

1) To find the verse location when you know a few words contained in the verse. For example, you may remember a portion of Scripture that says, "Submit yourselves therefore to God," but you can't cite the book, chapter and verse. By taking the main word, "Submit," and looking it up in a concordance, you will find out that the Scripture you want is James 4:7.

2) To find Bible contexts in which a certain word appears. Taking the word "submit" again, it is possible to find that the Bible enjoins Christians to:

1. Submit to one another (Ephesians 5:21).

2. Submit to God (James 4:7).

3. Wives, submit to their own husbands (Ephesians 5:22).

4. Submit to spiritual overseers (Hebrews 13:17).

5. Submit to every ordinance of man (I Peter 2:13).

A concordance, then, enables us to trace a given word through Scripture to see how it is used in a variety of contexts and what significance its usages have for us.

3) To find the original meaning of any word in the Bible. Although not every concordance provides this service, the larger concordances, *The Exhaustive Concordance of the Bible* by James Strong and the *Analytical Concordance to the Holy Bible* by Robert Young do offer this feature.

4) To learn how a certain Hebrew word or Greek word is translated in various ways in the English Bible. Again, either Young's or Strong's provides this service.

5) If you want to know how many different Hebrew or Greek words have been translated by the same English word, you may consult a thorough concordance, preferably Young's. For example, each of the words, "sin," "preach," and "servant," are translations of various Hebrew and Greek words having different shades of meaning. Awareness of these differences can enhance a teacher's ability to explain God's Word to others.

Bible Dictionary. A Bible dictionary lists alphabetically terms, places, objects, and persons mentioned in the Bible. Information, and sometimes pictures as well, are provided with each item. A teacher, puzzled by the word "chapiters" in Exodus 38:19 or the term "day of the Lord" in Joel 2:1, for example, may consult a Bible dictionary and gain the description he needs. Thus, a Bible dictionary is a must for any teacher's library.

Commentaries. Just as their name implies, commentaries make comments on the Scriptures, usually in verse-by-verse fashion. Several kinds of commentaries are available: single volume commentaries on the whole Bible, multiple volume sets of commentaries, and single volume commentaries on specific books of the Bible. A single volume commentary on the whole Bible is usually not thorough enough, so that when it is consulted for an explanation of a particularly difficult verse practically no comment is given. (It seems to be the style of so many single volume commentaries to treat the easy-to-understand verses and skip over the hard-to-understand ones.) A set of commentaries is often priced quite high, although the price is usually a worthwhile investment. A single volume commentary on a specific book of the Bible is probably the best investment of a teacher's money. A commentary on the Gospel of John, for example, can be bought at an affordable price and is likely to give more complete verse-by-verse information than either of the other kinds of commentaries.

These are the basic books for the teacher's library, but other books ought to be added as budget permits. In time, the teacher should purchase a Bible handbook, a good Bible introduction, Bible histories, archaeology books, theology books, Bible character studies, and any other books that would increase his knowledge of the Bible and sharpen his skills as a communicator of its truths.

CURRICULUM MATERIALS

Although some teachers of adults feel confident enough to prepare and present Sunday School lessons of their own composition, by and large it is advisable to use published curriculum materials. For one thing, they have been planned, written, and produced by experts in Christian education, communication and graphic arts. Therefore, they reflect an awareness of what adults want to study and need to study as well as an awareness of what facilitates the learning process.

Then, too, curriculum producers can devote their full-time thinking and skills to the task of providing teachers with the very best lessons and helps, whereas most teachers of adults do not have enough time to originate their own lessons and helps.

Finally, following a curriculum tends to guarantee students a more complete Bible coverage, because teachers who select their own lesson Scriptures often choose only those passages of Scripture that are most familiar to them.

Curriculum materials generally include a teacher's manual, a student manual, and teaching/learning resources like visuals and student response items. In making his selection of curriculum materials, a teacher ought to get well acquainted with every available item supplied by his publisher and use each as the publisher recommends.

AUDIOVISUALS

The list of available audiovisual resources has grown considerably in the last couple of decades, so that conceivably a Sunday School classroom could contain a wide assortment of audiovisual equipment from chalkboard to videotape. The following items, though, lie within reach of most teachers of adults and can help to maximize Bible learning.

Chalkboard. A large and portable chalkboard with reversible front and back slates can be one of the most helpful visual aids in a classroom. Lesson outlines, diagrams, sketches, definitions, lists, and many more items can be placed on a chalkboard to provide a simple but effective learning device. An eraser and plenty of chalk should be on hand for every class session.

Cassette Player. Although listening to a taped

lecture or discussion for a whole class session may bore most students, a cassette player can be put to good use. For example, at a crucial point in a lesson the teacher may play a brief dialogue between persons locked in a heated discussion about some issue, then ask the students for their views on which person, if either, had taken the right side of the issue. Taped opinions, commentaries, statements of problems for the class to try to solve Scripturally, and audio skits are some of the possibilities for using a cassette player in an adult class.

Overhead Projector and Transparencies. In recent years teachers of adults have turned in increasing numbers to the overhead projector. It is a versatile attention-getter and learning aid when it is used properly. The projected image should be clearly visible to the whole class. The teacher should use transparencies that are distinct, simple, and attractive. If the teacher writes on a transparency, he should not make his letters smaller than a quarter of an inch. Press-on letters, too, should be at least a quarter of an inch in size.

In showing a transparency, it is important to turn the overhead projector off as soon as the class has had enough time to view the image and hear the accompanying comments about it. Keeping it running beyond this point will divert the students' attention to the image instead of to the teacher and thereby obstruct the flow of communication.

Excellent transparencies related to Bible topics are on the market today, giving teachers a copious supply of colorful and educationally helpful visuals. Most Christian bookstores display sets of transparencies from which a selection may be made. Accent Publications has prepared sets of transparencies which are closely correlated with their adult Sunday School courses, so that teachers may enjoy using professionally prepared transparencies to reinforce almost every lesson they teach.

Maps. Large classroom maps of Bible lands can take the mystery out of Bible geography. Students can get the feel of Paul's travels when they view them on maps. The locations of Jesus' miracles mean something when they are shown on a map. Likewise, students can appreciate more fully the wilderness wanderings, the settlement of Israel in Canaan, the Divided Kingdom, the church's first-century missionary outreach, and the cities of the seven churches of Asia Minor when they see all of these on maps.

While these are the most commonly used audiovisuals in adult classes, others are worthy of consideration — charts, filmstrips, slides, short films, pictures, and television. Undoubtedly, technology will produce even more efficient audiovisual equipment as time progresses.

RESOURCE CARD FILE

In addition to the resources provided by curriculum materials a teacher may draw from his own source of poems, thoughts and illustrations. All it takes is a workable file. For years I have been building a poems, thoughts, illustrations file for my personal use in lesson preparation, having received the basic plan from Harold Garner who headed up the Christian Education Department at Moody Bible Institute when I was a student there from 1954 to 1957. Any teacher can build a similar file with a minimum of time and effort invested weekly or monthly.

The file consists of 8½-by-11-inch master sheets listing topics alphabetically and 3-by-5-inch file cards which store poems, thoughts, and illustrations related to

MASTER FILE: POEMS, THOUGHTS, ILLUSTRATIONS

A

Abiding	A-1
Abortion	A-2
Abounding	A-3
Absenteeism	A-4
Abundance	A-5
Acceptance	A-6
Accidents	A-7
Accumulation	A-8
Accuracy (of the Bible)	A-9
Accusations	A-10
Acknowledgements	A-11
Acquaintances	A-12
Acquittal	A-13
Activity (ies)	A-14
Acts of God	A-15
Addiction	A-16
Adjustments	A-17
Administration	A-18
Admiration	A-19
Adoption	A-20
Adoration	A-21
Adversity, Affliction	A-22
Advice	A-23
Affection	A-24
Aging	A-25
Agony	A-26
Alcohol	A-27
Alienation	A-28
Ailments	A-29
Alive	A-30
Ambassadors	A-31
Ancestors	A-32
Angels	A-33
Anger	A-34
Animals	A-35
Answered Prayer	A-36
Anticipation	A-37
Anti-Semitism	A-38
Anxiety	A-39
Apathy	A-40

Apostles	A-41
Apparel	A-42
Appreciation	A-43
Apprehension	A-44
Appropriation	A-45
Approval	A-46
Arguing	A-47
Ark of the Covenant	A-48
Ark (Noah's)	A-49
Arminianism	A-50
Armor	A-51
Ascension	A-52
Associations	A-53
Assumptions	A-54
Assurance	A-55
Astrology	A-56
Astronomy	A-57
Atheism	A-58
Athletics	A-59
Atomic	A-60
Atrocities	A-61
Attendance	A-62
Attitudes	A-63
Attributes	A-64
Authority of the Bible	A-65
Authorship of the Bible	A-66
Avarice	A-67
Awareness	A-68

B

Babies	B-1
Balance	B-2
Baptism	B-3
Basics	B-4
Battles	B-5
Beatitudes	B-6
Beauty	B-7

Figure 1. A sample master sheet of a poems, thoughts, illustrations file.

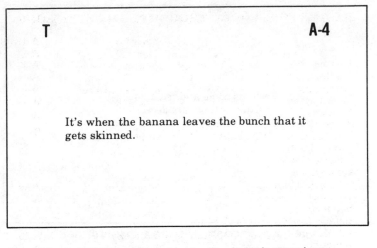

T   **A-4**

It's when the banana leaves the bunch that it
gets skinned.

Figure 2. A thought on church attendance is stored on a
file card.

I   **A-22**

A small boy's sailboat stalled in the middle of a
pond as the wind died. A big boy threw stones
at the sailboat, much to the small boy's dismay.
But each stone landed beyond the boat, caused
a ripple of water to float the boat closer to the
shore. Eventually, enough stones thrown
brought the sailboat within the small boy's
reach, and he understood that the big boy had
really shown kindness. If we think God is
throwing stones in our direction, we ought to
realize that they are carefully aimed to bring us
closer to Him.

Figure 3. An illustration of how adversity brings us
closer to God is stored on a file card.

Figure 4. A poem emphasizing the authority of the Bible is stored on a file card.

those topics. Figure 1 shows one of the master sheets I use. Figures 2, 3, and 4 show the kinds of things that can be placed on the file cards.

Each file card must have a code in the upper right corner, indicating the topic of the information stored on it. The letter in the upper left corner of the card indicates whether the information is a poem, a thought, or an illustration (P—poem, T—thought, I—illustration). Information may be typed on each file card, or it may be clipped from its source and attached by clear Scotch tape. If the information is lengthy, the clipped material may be folded and taped at its top to the card.

Having this kind of a resource file can help a teacher capture and maintain class interest by presenting a right-on-target poem, thought, or illustration at any given point in a lesson. Of course, a teacher's manual provides good illustrative material, but a teacher's own file permits him to add to or substitute for illustrations in the teacher's manual.

Gathering information for the resource card file is not hard, for sources abound almost everywhere — newspapers, magazines, Christian periodicals, sermons, TV news, radio, and the hundreds of situations in which a teacher finds himself in the course of daily living. But appropriate information can be passed over, forgotten and lost unless a teacher is alert enough to capture it and secure it for a session of getting it stored on cards and filed away for just the right time when it will come in handy. So carrying a notebook and pencil at all times is a good habit to form.

Just as acquiring tools in any trade costs something and demands building a good supply over a period of time, even so there is an investment of money and time to be made by the teacher who wants to acquire the tools of the teaching trade. But the investment is worthwhile, for when the tools are used to shape students' lives for the glory of God the workman's personal satisfaction is beyond compare.

QUICK REVIEW

1. A teacher should study only a Bible that has nothing but the text of Scripture, because this is the best way to be taught by the Holy Spirit.   T   F

2. A Bible concordance lists alphabetically the main words of the Bible.   T   F

3. A Bible dictionary's main purpose is to help Bible students with the spelling of names and places in the Bible.   T   F

4. It is advisable for a teacher of adults to use curriculum materials supplied by a publisher.   T   F

5. Letters on a transparency should not be smaller than a quarter of an inch.   T   F

6. For best results a teacher should not leave an overhead projector on when he is no longer referring to its visual. T   F

7. Anyone can build a resource card file. T F
8. A resource card file utilizes master sheets. T F

7 Teaching Methods

To some extent we are all creatures of habit. We wake up at the usual hour, get out of the same side of the bed, go through a predictable routine for dressing, grooming, eating and leaving the house for work. Generally, we take the same route and transportation to work day after day, follow standard procedures on the job, leave for home at an established time, go home the usual way, and spend the evening almost hour for hour the way we have spent hundreds of other evenings. Saturdays and Sundays provide a break in our week, but even then we follow a rather predictable *modus operandi*.

Take Sunday, for example. We have a Sunday rising time, usual Sunday breakfast, head out for Sunday School and church at a prescribed time, arriving at about the same time as certain familiar acquaintances, and follow a kind of ritual for commencing the Sunday School hour. (Sometimes the ritual is called "Opening Exercises," although the only exercise involved is standing to sing a couple of very familiar songs, maybe smile and shake hands with a few friends around us, and march off to our classes.)

Now, there's nothing intrinsically wrong with following a routine if it is a helpful routine and doesn't become a rut from which escape seems impossible and in which we are oblivious to better ways of doing things. As someone has observed, "A rut is simply a grave with the ends kicked out." And nowhere is a rut more noticeable and counterproductive than in an adult Sunday School class where the teacher uses the same teaching method every Sunday! If variety is the spice of life, it is equally the spice of teaching. Drawing from the following teaching methods will help a teacher to serve up a zesty lesson every Sunday.

LECTURE

Although the lecture method of teaching has fallen into widespread disfavor among many Christian educators, we shouldn't rule out the possibility that it can serve both teacher and students well. One of the phenomena of our lifetime is the appeal of a certain Bible teacher's seminars. Those who attend — and the number is multitudinous — sit for hours listening to lectures presented with the aid of an overhead projector. Teacher-centered learning? Absolutely! Content-oriented? Indeed! Old-fashioned method? Yes! Dull and a waste of the students' time? Not at all! As a matter of fact, students take notes feverishly and insist long after the seminars have ended that the whole experience was the most helpful thing that ever happened to them. So, the lecture method can work well in the hands of a capable teacher. A lot depends upon what is said, how it is said, who is saying it (speaker prestige goes a long way toward making a lecture interesting), how long the lecture lasts, and how motivated the listeners are to derive help from it.

So let's not rule out the lecture method altogether. I am convinced that in some classes the lecture method is getting an effective job accomplished, for I have been told by some teachers and their classes that it is working well for them, far better than anything else.

The problem is, of course, that quite a few teachers do not lecture well, and consequently their classes lack vitality, warmth and growth.

I have visited adult classes where a teacher's lecture resembled a mild form of punishment. As he stared blankly at his notes on the podium or at a grease spot about eighteen inches above the clock on the back wall, the students stared blankly at the floor and shuffled their feet back and forth as if they felt that would make the time pass less painfully. Occasionally, an adult whispered to a neighbor that he was slipping out early to see whether the Sunday School treasurer needed help counting the offering. And another excused herself quietly by claiming that she thought she heard a familiar cry coming from the nursery. In such cases, I doubt that much learning was accomplished. The students were passive — almost unconscious — and the teacher was on the verge of self-induced sleep.

A teacher who sincerely wants to know whether his lecturing is effective may ask his class for their honest opinion. He may set before them a few choices. Do they feel they are benefiting from the lectures, or would they prefer some other class time formats?

An alternative to exposing the lecture method to the students' vote is the pre-test, post-test system. At the beginning of a class session, a teacher gives an objective test on the subject he plans to lecture about. After the lecture, he gives the same test again. By comparing the test results he is able to determine whether there was significant improvement in the students' knowledge of the subject as a result of his lecture. If this sounds like too much emphasis on the students' ability to accumulate facts during the course of a lecture, let me say that the lecture method may also be tested on its effectiveness in changing attitudes. The pre-test may be structured as an attitudes survey. After the lecture, it is given again as a post-test. By comparing the two, the teacher sees how much attitudes changed during the lecture.

There are ways to improve lecturing. Since student attention usually sags in the middle of most lectures, a teacher may help the situation by taking a break in the middle for student feedback. Indeed, dividing the lecture into several sections, with some student involvement at the close of each section, can aid the lecture method considerably. Writing on the lecture method, John McLeish observes in *The Psychology of Teaching Methods,* (The National Society for the Study of Education, 1976, p. 301):

> The "middle sag" in attention and recall points to the need for a diversification of activities during the lecture period so that it ceases to be an uninterrupted discourse by one person, performed face-to-face with a passive audience. The principles of programmed learning, and learning theory in general, suggest that the best way to improve the lecture is to convert it into a step-by-step presentation with perhaps half-a-dozen intervals of recapitulation and informal testing of the students' assimilation and ability to apply the material presented.

During his lecture the teacher may facilitate the learning process by maintaining eye contact with his students, as we observed in chapter 5. There is nothing more frustrating for students than to have to look at a teacher who isn't looking at them. The lack of eye contact makes them feel that their presence in the classroom is not essential in the least. The teacher might just as well be delivering his lecture in an isolation chamber.

If this frustration continues for very long, the students will likely start looking for a different Sunday School and church. Or they might decide to stay home during Sunday School. By maintaining eye contact, the teacher can spare his class all this frustration. And, if he complements the eye contact with mobility and appropriate visuals, his lecturing can become captivating.

Generally, in using the lecture method, the teacher gives his students the main lesson, but he can enhance the effectiveness of this presentation by incorporating other teaching methods into the class session. Any of the methods described in the rest of this chapter and in chapters 8 and 9 — or a combination of them — may be combined with lecturing for an innovative and productive change of pace.

DISCUSSION

For some teachers of adults, leading a discussion is more difficult than lecturing. But a few basic principles, kept firmly in mind, can make discussion an enjoyable and very effective teaching method. We shall examine these one at a time.

1) *For effective discussion the teacher should explain the purpose of the discussion.* Is it to discuss an issue? Solve a problem? Learn how the group members have implemented a certain Bible principle in a difficult situation? Determine how a passage of Scripture relates to daily living? Draw comparisons between a Bible character and modern-day Christians? Once the purpose has been stated clearly and everyone in the class understands it the tendency to ramble and get off the track is reduced. If "rabbit chasing" does occur, it is easy enough for the teacher to bring the class back to the main topic. A simple "Before we travel too far in that direction,

I think we had better get back to the real purpose of our discussion" will regain control of the discussion.

It is absolutely essential to state a purpose and to stay with it. Without this kind of direction, class discussion will resemble a ship without a compass, sailing along at the mercy of the wind without much, if any, say-so about where the wind is taking it. In leading a discussion, keep in mind that just sitting around talking may be a pleasant experience but accomplishes nothing unless clear direction has been given and sustained. Most adults want to leave Sunday School feeling that they have contributed and received spiritual help. They attend Sunday School for more than a friendly chat!

2) *As the discussion leader, the teacher must guide the discussion flow.* Unlike the lecture method, where the teacher does the talking and the students listen, the discussion method functions best when free-flowing communication takes place among the students with the teacher acting as a "traffic director." Several things can promote this kind of activity.

Seating Arrangement. Have you been in a meeting or class session where the teacher or leader stood in front of the group seated in rows facing him, and the format was supposed to be group discussion? Frustrating, wasn't it? People near the back of the room couldn't hear what those up near the front were saying. And people near the front couldn't hear or see those at the back. Let's face it, staring at the back of heads or having the back of your head stared at just isn't conducive to good discussion, especially when people have difficulty hearing one another's comments and questions.

Fortunately, there is a better way to arrange the seating. Figure 1 shows the traditional arrangement, which serves the purpose of the lecture method but is very poor for discussion. Figure 2 shows the kind of seating that is helpful in holding class discussion.

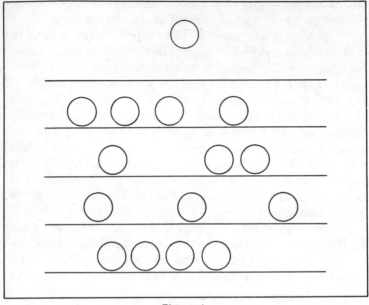

Figure 1.
Poor seating arrangement for
discussion group.

Notice in Figure 2 that no one sits outside the circle, the teacher sits in the circle with the rest of the class, and no one is looking at the back of anyone's head. This means: 1) since no one is outside the circle, no one is cast in the role of an observer or a critic; 2) the discussion leader is accepted as a participant rather than regarded as an authority; and 3) each member of the class can see the faces of the rest of the class, making it easier to give and receive messages throughout the class.

Restraint. For communication to flow effectively around the class, the discussion leader must exercise self-restraint. He must not serve as the answer man, replying to every question a student raises. He must not interrupt the discussion frequently in order to interject

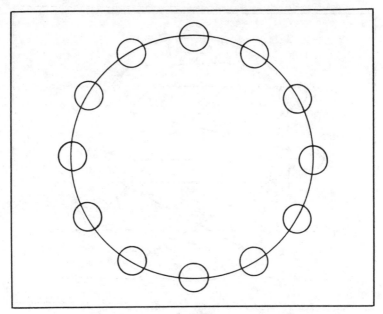

Figure 2.
Good seating arrangement for
discussion group.

his opinions. Nor should he say something in response to each comment the students make. Restraint on his part will help to produce the kind of communication flow illustrated by Figure 3. Lack of restraint would most likely produce the situation illustrated by Figure 4.

There are times, of course, when the discussion leader ought to assert himself. As I previously mentioned, he should pull the group back to their main purpose whenever they get off on tangents. At other times he may need to help the students to clarify their comments, reword their questions, define their terms, and restate their findings. The key word in all of this, as far as the discussion leader is concerned, is *control* not *dominate*.

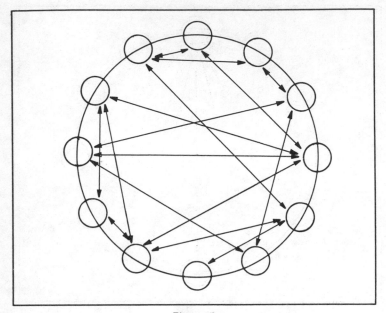

Figure 3.
Good communication.

Drawing as many as possible into the discussion. A group discussion will fall flat on its face if only two or three persons express themselves. Ideally, everyone in the group should share in the discussion (as per Figure 3).

This calls for a skillful touch on the part of the discussion leader. He may arrange the seating in a way that will encourage everyone to participate. Talkers should be seated opposite non-talkers, since students are most likely to address those who sit across from them. This will pull the non-talkers into the conversation. Also, it is wise to separate close friends so that whispering among neighbors will be kept to a minimum. If necessary, place name tags on the chairs before your students arrive for class. Letting the quieter students

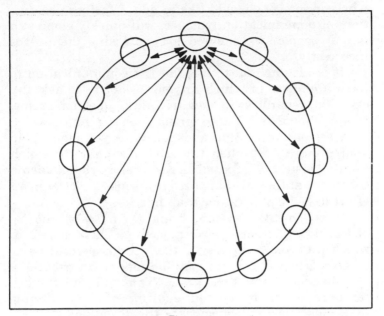

Figure 4.
Poor communication.

know that their input is valuable will also increase the flow of communication.

When you see that certain students are sitting on the sidelines, say something like: "Bill, I'm sure you have an interesting thought on this. How about sharing it with us?" Or, "Helen, you look like you want to ask a question at this point." Or, "Ted, have you had an experience along this line? We'd like to hear from you."

When students enter into the discussion, recognize their contribution by complimenting them on their good thinking and praising them for their interesting comments. If someone makes a comment that is off-base doctrinally or ethically, don't censure him or ridicule him. Simply say (if you feel you must say something), "Thanks for expressing your opinion, Joe. I wonder whether someone would like to add a further observation." Communication, you see, will quickly come to a halt if people are censured for expressing themselves incorrectly.

It is also helpful to free-flowing communication to have a climate in which anyone feels free to ask any question, regardless of how trivial the question seems. No one should be ridiculed for not knowing the answer to what seems like a simple question. Also, you should help your group to establish the kind of climate in which arguing is next to impossible. Keep before your students the fact that they are supposed to discuss a matter in an effort to be helpful rather than hurtful.

If arguments develop, bring them to a stop by observing that some strong feelings have emerged, which call for a break in the action, permitting a recapitulation of the group's findings or contributions by other members of the group. This will give the hot tempers a much needed cooling off period and reestablish the main purpose of the discussion.

The Right Kinds of Questions. Communication flow can be stopped or helped depending upon the kinds of questions you provide as discussion starters. Avoid those that call for a simple "yes" or "no" or some other one-word answer. Try to pose questions that investigate the reasons why certain things happened to Bible characters, how God worked in their lives, how they responded, why those responses were or were not appropriate.

Ask how Bible truths relate to our lives. Ask questions that probe feelings, unearth opinions, confront students with decisions. In brief, shape your questions into surgical instruments that penetrate deep into your students' thinking, emotions, and will, so that they stimulate them to approach life with Bible truth that makes a difference in their philosophy of life and their total life-style.

3) *As discussion leader, the teacher must help the class to summarize the discussion and draw conclusions.* It would be disappointing to end a discussion period without recapping the main points of the discussion and gathering the conclusions which could help the students to meet the challenges of the coming week. So a brief but thorough wrap-up is essential. As the teacher, you may wish to provide this wrap-up; but often it may be best to let your adults list the summary points and conclusions. Listing these on a chalkboard is a good way to reinforce them in your adults' thinking.

Undoubtedly, the discussion method has gained a great deal of popularity in recent years, perhaps because of the values inherent in it. In *Helping the Teacher* (Broadman Press, 1959, p. 98) Findley B. Edge lists five values of the discussion method: 1) It leads the members to become aware of and face some of the problems they need to face as Christians. 2) It enables a person to gain new information and deeper insights from the views expressed by fellow class members and the teacher. 3) It gives an individual the opportunity to study the Bible in terms of the problem he is facing in life. 4) It gives him an opportunity to express and clarify his own views in the light of the total class discussion. 5) It gives him an opportunity to evaluate and perhaps revise his own views in the light of the total discussion.

THE QUESTION AND ANSWER METHOD

Also called the recitation method, the question and answer method of teaching was employed extensively in the Old Testament and New Testament eras. Jewish youth received their education by this system. Likely Luke 2:46,47 gives us a glimpse at this method as we see the boy Jesus in the temple conversing with the Jewish theologians. We read: "And it came to pass, that after three days they found him in the midst of the doctors, both hearing them, and asking them questions. And all that heard him were astonished at his understanding and answers." It seems the question and answer method was employed by both Jesus and the theologians on this occasion.

This method provides a way for the teacher to determine how much factual knowledge his students have acquired in a subject. And it provides the students with an opportunity to work independently, studying the subject matter diligently. Naturally, the question and answer method will fall flat on its face unless the teacher assigns work to the students ahead of the class session in which the testing is to take place. And a lot depends, too, upon the type of questions that will be asked. Each question must derive its answer from the assigned readings. It must be phrased in clear language. Trick questions are totally out of place. Also, a question should not include two or more elements so that students aren't forced to wonder which part or parts of the question they are supposed to answer.

Nearly every adult class has one or two students who are loaded with factual Bible knowledge. Their tendency is to try to answer every question before anyone else has an opportunity to do so. A wise teacher in such a case will tell the class that he wants as many students as possible to participate in answering the questions. He will likely limit a person to answering only three or four questions correctly during a class session. Or he will call upon students by name to answer the questions. If he chooses this last system, he ought to be careful to call out the student's name and get his attention before he poses the question. It can be embarrassing when a student is called upon to answer a question he didn't hear because of inattention.

The question and answer method can accomplish more than the recall of information if the teacher structures his questions in a way that compels students to relate Bible information to real-life situations. The following are samples of such questions:

- What does this mean to you personally?
- On the basis of the information contained in this passage of Scripture, how would you advise a person facing the following situation . . . ?
- What implications do you see here for Christian living?
- How has this passage of Scripture changed your outlook on life?
- How will you live differently because of the knowledge you have gained from this study?

With a little imagination a teacher can turn the question and answer method into a very enjoyable learning experience. The class can divide into several quiz teams and compete to see which team scores highest in the questioning. Another variation would establish a game format, similar to a TV game show format. For example, persons could compete in a Tic Tac Toe contest. In order to place his X or 0 a contestant would have to answer a question correctly. Or a quiz game resembling Jeopardy could be devised. All that is necessary is dividing the questions into categories with a series of points attached to the questions in each category. The contestants would simply choose a category and point value in selecting each question. Of course, the one with the most points at the close of the contest is the winner.

Further use of the question and answer method could include asking the adults to write brief answers to a series of opinion questions. Later, they would be asked to search the Lesson Scripture to determine whether it supported or contradicted each of their opinions. This exercise helps students to yield their opinions (and biases) to the authority of Scripture.

One final idea regarding the question and answer method — why not permit the students themselves the opportunity once in a while to prepare their own set of questions on the subject matter under study? They could take turns in class presenting their questions to the class. The exercise involved in preparing the questions would help the students to acquire Bible study habits, and the exchange of questions in class could be an enjoyable change of pace.

QUICK REVIEW

1. It is always wrong to lecture to an adult class. T F

2. Pre-testing and post-testing can help a teacher evaluate the effectiveness of his lecturing.   T F

3. Dividing a lecture into sections with student involvement between sections can aid the lecture method.   T F

4. Non-directed discussion is best for use with adults.   T F

5. Seating arrangement can help or hurt the discussion method.   T F

6. In a discussion group, close friends ought to be seated next to each other.   T F

7. One advantage of the discussion method is the teacher doesn't have to prepare for the class session.   T F

8. Likely, the question and answer method was involved in Jesus' episode with the religious leaders in the Temple (Luke 2:46,47).   T F

9. Occasionally, it would be a good idea for students to prepare sets of questions on a lesson.   T F

10. Trick questions should be included in every quiz.

                                                          T F

Answers:
1. F 2. T 3. T 4. F 5. T 6. F 7. F 8. T 9. T 10. F

8 More Teaching Methods

In this chapter we shall continue our discussion of the variety of teaching methods which are available to the teacher of adults. By selecting his methods carefully and varying their use, a teacher will set the stage for enjoyable and successful learning week after week.

SKITS AND PANTOMIMES

Drama with or without dialogue can effectively capture student interest and assist the learning process. Sometimes we fail to see a truth unless it is emphatically acted out in front of us. Then we understand it more fully and respond to it more appropriately. For example, the following brief skit, designed to involve two female class members, derives from a lesson on James, chapter 3, and emphasizes the truth that we need to control the tongue. The "actresses" use toy phones and stage the following conversation.

MILLY: Hi, Betty. How are you?
BETTY: Oh, pretty good, Milly, considering what went on at church yesterday. You know how things can irritate a person there these days.

MILLY: You said it! Ever since that new pastor arrived I haven't had a decent Sunday. I didn't vote for him, you know. And I sure can't understand why most of the church members did. I guess there are more ignorant people in our church than I realized. I mean ... how dumb can people be?

BETTY: I know just what you mean, Milly. I didn't vote for him either. For one thing, I couldn't stand the way he was dressed when he candidated. I think he must have bought his suit for $5 at the Good Hand-Me-Downs store. And his taste for clothes hasn't improved one bit since he became our pastor. I can hardly force myself to look at him when he preaches.

MILLY: I have the same problem. But what bothers me more is the way his wife dresses. She probably considers a trip to a rummage sale as a day out on the town.

BETTY: Well, as I was saying, I had a bad day at church last Sunday. You know how much I detest that Frieda Flossinger ever since she became President of the Ladies Auxiliary — a position I was in line for. Well, you can imagine how I felt when I read in the church bulletin that she was the scheduled soloist for the morning service. When she sang, I felt like yelling "Boo." I probably would have if I wasn't such a committed Christian.

MILLY: I wouldn't have blamed you, Betty. You surely showed a lot of grace not to boo. After all, everyone should realize that Frieda is anything but a good Christian. She's certainly not the kind of person who should take part in a worship service. Rumor has it that she treats her husband just awful.

BETTY: That's what I've heard too. Frieda's poor husband does look undernourished. She must starve the poor soul. I noticed on Sunday that he looks like warmed-over death.

MILLY: Maybe Frieda sings around the house, Betty. You know that voice of hers may be hazardous to her husband's health. Maybe he's suffering from shock.

Anyhow, what else was bad about last Sunday?

BETTY: The Brewsters sat right in front of me. You know who they are, don't you?

MILLY: Used to attend our church a couple of years ago, didn't they?

BETTY: That's right. I thought when they left that it was good riddance to bad rubbish. Troublemakers, that's what they were. You know, they had the nerve once to stand up in a business meeting and suggest that we transfer the funds from the trash compressor account to missions. Some people don't have any respect for the environment. Another time they opposed me in a business session when I suggested that it was about time for the pastor to move to a different pasture. The church attendance wasn't growing very fast, you know. Well, the Brewsters got right up in that meeting and suggested that the church members do some calling in the neighborhood to help build up the attendance. They said the church needed a visitation program, and they offered to be the first to sign up for it. Anyhow, when Mr. Big-Mouth Brewster got a job transfer and they moved out of town, believe me, I didn't shed a single tear when the church sang, "God be with you till we meet again." Little did I realize how soon we would meet again — like last Sunday. Seems they've moved back into town.

MILLY: Know what you mean, Betty. If there's one thing our church doesn't need, it's a couple of busybodies like the Brewsters. Well, gotta hang up now; I'm expecting my mother-in-law for lunch. When she leaves, I'll be over to share an Alka-Seltzer with you.

BETTY: Okay. So long, Milly.

MILLY: So long. (Hangs up.) Wow, what a miserable person to talk to.

BETTY (Hangs up): After a terrible Sunday that's all I needed — a call from Milly, the town crier!

A skit could be followed by a series of penetrating

questions. This would help the students to relate the main truths communicated by the skit to their own situations. For example, here are several follow-up questions for the telephone skit.

- Do you believe a little bit of gossip is harmless? Why?
- Why do you agree or disagree that it takes at least two persons to give gossip a "good" start?
- What steps can a Christian take to minimize gossip?
- How can you squelch gossip when someone tries to gossip to you?
- What does James, chapter 3, have to say to Milly and Betty?
- What help does James, chapter 3, give us for controlling the tongue?

But you may consider script writing too difficult a task and decide to rule out the use of skits as a teaching device. Don't be too hasty. Let it be known that you can use the writing talents of adults in your class, and don't be surprised to find a few capable writers emerge to give you excellent scripts for skits. Also, you can expect to uncover some acting ability among your adults. Consequently, more students will be actively involved in making Sunday School a successful, enjoyable experience.

Some things can be acted out without words, of course. This is where pantomime serves a worthwhile purpose. Use it from time to time as an interesting and unusual alternative teaching tool.

MODELING

Sometimes modeling is called imitative, vicarious, or observational learning. It consists of observing someone doing something in a proficient manner, then imitating that behavior until the observer develops similar proficiency. Actually, from childhood modeling has been a part of life and an important contributor to the learning process. Learning how to walk was dependent to a great extent upon imitating parents. By imitating a teacher's handwriting, we learned to write. Driving skill was developed in part by observing an experienced driver operate a vehicle. Gaining ability in task after task was dependent upon following the example of an appropriate model. Why, then, should we not use modeling to good advantage in the adult Sunday School class? The modeling method of teaching can serve our adults well.

For example, your class may include an adult who has experienced great success in winning people to Christ. Obviously, he or she possesses a skill that the rest of the adults in your class would like to have. This is where the modeling method can fit into your class session. By simulating occasions involving the soul-winning student and various unsaved persons, your adults can observe effective methods of winning people to Christ. They may see how the soul winner relates to each person and leads him to saving faith in Christ. Various kinds of unsaved people may be portrayed by members of your class: the skeptic, the religious do-gooder, the person who has had no religious training, etc. After observing the soul winner in action, students should try to practice the skills they observed during the simulations.

Modeling becomes increasingly effective when the students establish definite goals, attain them, and encounter satisfying results. In the case of the modeled soul-winning skills, the students ought to set soul-winning goals for themselves. One student may decide that his goal will be to witness to one person during the week. Another may establish his goal as winning one person to Christ in the coming month. Another may decide upon two persons won to Christ in the coming week as his goal.

The teacher would be unwise to establish any goal for any student without the student's accepting it as the goal he wants to reach. If the students reach the goals they have set (and they should be encouraged to set realistic, achievable goals), the satisfaction they derive from accomplishing these goals, coupled with sincere and generous praise from you, their teacher, will encourage them to set further goals and strive to attain them. Eventually, soul winning will be an integral part of their Christian living.

Other valuable skills which can be communicated effectively by the modeling method include:

- Discipling a new believer
- Inviting someone to Sunday School and church
- Visiting the ill
- Visiting newcomers
- Welcoming visitors
- Bible study (the model explains what he is doing as he does it)
- Bible teaching
- Presenting a devotional talk

Using models to demonstrate effective behavior is not limited to live presentations. Short films, slides, audiotapes may be utilized to depict the kinds of behavior you want your students to learn and adopt.

ROLE PLAYING

In his very practical and helpful book, *Communication for the Church,* Raymond W. McLaughlin defines role playing as "an individual acting endeavor put on by a member of the group in the larger production called sociodrama." According to McLaughlin, "All of this is done extemporaneously without script or conscious effort for artistic effect." Findley B. Edge, in *Helping the Teacher,* gives a similar definition. He states: "Role playing is an adaptation of . . . 'make believe play,' in which the class may observe various attitudes expressed and evaluate the consequences of those attitudes. It is a brief, spontaneous, unrehearsed presentation of a problem in which certain members of the class act out certain roles. There is no script prepared, no memorizing of parts."

Role playing gives adults an opportunity to see how real-life situations can be helped by applying Biblical directives and principles to those situations. And there is practically no limit to the kinds of situations that may be analyzed in this way.

Usually, role playing fits into a class session within the following pattern:

1. The class studies a passage of Scripture which deals with principles or commands for a certain situation. For example, the passage may be Colossians 3:12-15:

> "Put on therefore, as the elect of God, holy
> and beloved, bowels of mercies, kindness,
> humbleness of mind, meekness, long-
> suffering;
>
> "Forbearing one another, and forgiving
> one another, if any man have a quarrel
> against any: even as Christ forgave you,
> so also do ye.
>
> "And above all these things put on
> charity, which is the bond of perfectness.
>
> "And let the peace of God rule in your
> hearts, to the which also ye are called in
> one body; and be ye thankful."

Obviously, this passage has something to say about Christians getting along together, practicing forgiveness, kindness, mutual help, self-control and patience. According to the passage, believers should exercise the same kind of forgiveness Christ exhibited in forgiving us. Furthermore, believers should demonstrate a spirit of peace and unity.

2. The teacher leads the class in considering how this passage of Scripture relates to a problem. He identifies the problem he has in mind. The setting is a church business meeting in which the moderator has introduced a trustees' recommendation that the church remodel the kitchen at a cost of $6,000. It so happens that the Chairman of the Trustees Committee and Mr. Z, a church member, are longtime foes. Furthermore, Mr. Z feels strongly that the present kitchen can serve the church's needs for at least another ten years. He would rather see the $6,000 applied to the purchase of an organ. He gains the floor and presents his case. The Chairman of the Trustees Committee replies to Mr. Z instantly, and before long the two are involved in a heated argument.

3. The teacher selects two class members to assume the roles of Mr. Z and the Chairman of the Trustees Committee.

4. The role playing proceeds. Both players say and do precisely what they feel Mr. Z and the Chairman of the Trustees Committee would say and do in the business meeting.

5. When the teacher feels that the role playing has gone on long enough, he calls a halt to it and thanks the class members for their participation.

6. The class discusses what went on between Mr. Z and the Chairman of the Trustees Committee. They consider what they did wrong or right, how their actions and words related to Colossians 3:12-15, and how they might have resolved their differences (if they did not) in a manner that would concur with the teaching of

Colossians 3:12-15.

7. The role playing is repeated, but this time the actors resolve the dispute in a charitable manner that concurs with the teaching of Colossians 3:12-15.

8. The class draws final conclusions about appropriate behavior when the unity of believers is at stake.

Occasionally, in role playing the actors may reverse roles for a look at the other person's point of view. In the situation involving Mr. Z and the Chairman of the Trustees Committee a reversal of roles, followed by class discussion, could lead to a dramatic solution to the problem.

As you develop a sensitivity to the role playing method, you will recognize many situations which could benefit from its classroom use. The following are just a few of these situations:

- A family dispute over TV program selections.
- A husband-wife argument over budget items.
- A father-mother spat over child-care responsibilities.
- A family dispute over whether or not to attend Prayer Meeting.
- A troubled mother and father dealing with a teenage daughter or son who has come home very late from a date.
- A quarrel between parents and their teen over the teen's penchant for rock music.
- An overbearing employer telling off a Christian employee who is innocent of the charge.
- A dispute between a Christian and his non-Christian neighbor over the building of a high fence.
- An overzealous Christian pinning down a disinterested non-Christian in a witnessing effort.
- An encounter between an atheist and a Christian.
- A gossiping session.
- A church recruiter trying to enlist a reluctant

church member for visitation night.

Because role playing depends upon the involvement of outgoing, uninhibited adults, you may find that only a few persons in your class are willing to serve as actors. Rather than having the same persons role playing too often, you may want to restrict this method to just a few class sessions each quarter. However, when you use it, expect your class to really come alive.

QUICK REVIEW

1. It might help a skit's effectiveness to ask questions about it following the performance.   T F

2. Modeling's effectiveness depends in part upon the human tendency to imitate.   T F

3. Behavioral goals will most likely fail unless students accept them as their personal goals.   T F

4. Goals should be realistic; that is, they should lie within the students' ability to reach them.   T F

5. Role playing ought to be rehearsed carefully, using a complete script.   T F

6. Role playing can help students to solve problems. T F

7. It is all right for a teacher to stop the role playing when he feels it has gone on long enough.   T F

Answers:
1.T 2.T 3.T 4.T 5.F 6.T 7.T

9 Still More
Teaching Methods

The variety of teaching methods available to the teacher of adults is almost endless, limited only by finite imagination and human ingenuity. In this final chapter on teaching methods we shall consider a few more that lie on the surface of the educational counter, waiting to be picked up and tried out.

BUZZ GROUPS

A variation of the discussion method, the use of buzz groups to explore an urgent question or life-issue can stimulate students to think clearly and help one another to come to significant conclusions. Here's how it works:

1. The teacher raises a question while the whole class is assembled. The question, of course, ought to derive from the Lesson Scripture, or at least be directly related to it. Often, the teacher's manual or the student's study guide will list thought-provoking questions from which the teacher may make his selection.

2. The class divides into small groups to discuss the question. If the class is seated on portable chairs, forming buzz groups is easy. About half a dozen students, comprising each group, arrange their chairs in

a circle. If the class sits in pews or on chairs fastened to the floor, they must spread themselves around the room in cluster groups, or find available small rooms where they can meet.

3. Each buzz group selects a secretary/reporter who writes down the group's main thoughts and conclusions for sharing later with the entire class.

4. At the close of the allotted time for buzz group discussion, the groups assemble again as a class.

5. One by one, the secretary/reporters share their groups' observations and conclusions.

6. The entire class interacts further by asking questions related to the buzz groups' observations and conclusions and by discussing some matters further.

7. The teacher helps the class to summarize key points and make final application.

The following diagrams illustrate this useful teaching method.

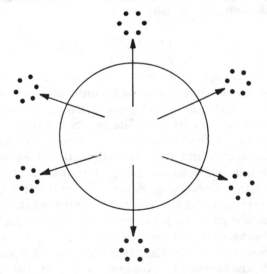

Diagram 1. The class divides into buzz groups to discuss a question or life-issue.

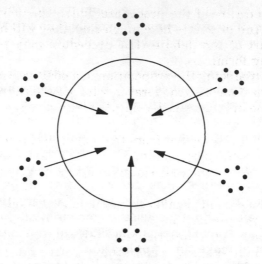

Diagram 2. The buzz groups return to class to report their observations and conclusions, and to enter into final summary and application.

DEBATE

Debate involves at least two persons, but usually four, who assume opposing viewpoints on an issue. Each side tries to persuade the other side that its viewpoint is the correct one. Although this method can produce a lively class session and get everyone thinking hard about important matters, it can also arouse tempers among debaters. So, in choosing men and women for the debate teams, look for persons who can express their personal convictions forcefully without permitting their emotions to carry them where angels fear to tread.

For best results, choose the debaters well in advance of the class session in which the debate will take place. Let them know what the topic is when you ask them to participate. Ask each person to defend the side of the issue he or she believes to be the correct side. Make sure they are aware of the procedure which the debate will follow. And stipulate how much time they will have for each part of the debate. The procedure may take the following form:

1. Introducing the proposition in a positive way. This should be done by a moderator, who may be the teacher.

2. The first affirmative speaker tells why he supports the proposition.

3. The first speaker from the negative side tells why he opposes the proposition.

4. The second affirmative speaker defends the proposition.

5. The second speaker from the negative side argues against the proposition.

6. Each team confers before the rebuttal.

7. The first speaker from the negative side presents his rebuttal.

8. The first speaker from the positive side presents his rebuttal.

9. The second speaker from the negative side gives his rebuttal.

10. The second speaker from the positive side gives his rebuttal.

The following topics are just a sample of the many that lend themselves well to the debating method. Likely others will come to your mind each quarter when you study the curriculum tools for long-range lesson planning.

- Abortion
- Social drinking
- Enrolling children in a Christian school
- Corporal punishment as a form of discipline
- Standards of attire and hairstyle
- Modern translations
- The purpose and duration of the sign gifts
- Non-Christian and Christian companionship
- Marriage between a believer and an unbeliever

- Ecumenism
- Divorce and remarriage
- The Christian and military service
- Cremation
- The prophetic time of the rapture
- Mode of baptism
- The Christian and labor unions
- The Christian's involvement in politics
- Ordination of women
- The role of divorcees in the church
- Cooperative evangelism
- Christian rock music
- Fund-raising events to support the church
- The church's obligation to the world's poor
- The church's obligation to its own poor
- Separation of church and state
- Tithing
- The eternal destiny of the heathen

PANEL DISCUSSION

A moderator (perhaps the teacher) and a few class members serve on a panel to discuss a topic. The discussion is rather free-flowing and generally unrehearsed. The moderator usually asks a number of questions throughout the panel discussion, sometimes directing them to specific panel members and at other times placing them before the entire panel. Each person presents his views and asks questions in a conversational style. The moderator closes the panel discussion by drawing together the participants' conclusions. He may also allow questions and comments from the class.

For the sake of variety, a teacher might decide to use the panel discussion method after lecturing to the class. This would provide the students with an excellent opportunity to discuss not only the lesson content but also ways to apply the lesson. And it would afford the teacher an opportunity to evaluate the effectiveness of his lecture.

Selecting panel members can be spontaneous, but it seems best to select them at least one week in advance and alert them to the subject matter they will discuss. Several carefully prepared questions by the moderator, given to them a few days before the panel discussion takes place, will increase the possibility that the panel discussion will be successful.

FORUM

This method consists of the entire class asking questions of the teacher after his lesson presentation. They may also express their opinions at this time. When adults know that a forum is scheduled, they have a good reason to listen closely to the teacher's lesson presentation. They want to participate in the forum by asking intelligent questions and offering helpful comments.

SYMPOSIUM

A symposium resembles a forum, but as Raymond McLaughlin points out in *Communication for the Church,* it "usually involves a panel of experts who have prepared formal speeches on various phases of a given problem. Audience participation is encouraged through the use of the question and answer period after the formal presentation."

You may not be able to import a panel of experts into your adult class, but don't rule out the symposium method. Two or three of your adults could be assigned areas of the lesson to study thoroughly. They would become "experts" in those areas and speak concerning those areas during the class session. Following their talks, the class would hold a symposium.

BRAINSTORMING

Somewhat similar to group discussion, brainstorming gives everyone who wants to share an opportunity to do so. There's only one rule: no negative comments are allowed. This means no Bronx cheering, no criticizing of what anyone says, no arguing against any idea, no ridiculing of even the most unlikely ideas. After all the ideas have been presented, a committee may study them, throwing out the unusable ones and retaining the best ideas for implementation.

You can see how brainstorming can be used as a follow-up procedure to any lesson that challenges Christians to make some life-action responses. For example, a lesson on John 4, dealing with the task of reaching out to others with the gospel, leads naturally into a brainstorming session on how to accomplish this in an effective way. The class may originate lots of ideas that can be turned over to your church's Evangelism Committee.

PROJECTS

Whether it's constructing a model of the Tabernacle, tracing genealogies, recording Jesus' miracles, or mapping Paul's travels, a project can create interest and give your adults new insights. There is always a risk, of course, that they will learn more from projects about how to construct models, chart genealogies, and draw maps than they will learn about the Bible subjects upon which the projects are based. The risk, however, shouldn't scare a teacher away from using the project method.

PROBLEM-SOLVING

Although no two people are exactly alike, people often face similar problems. So the experience of trying to solve problems during a class session can stand adults in good stead when they tackle similar problems in their own lives. Of course, the goal in this technique is solving problems through the effective application of Biblical principles.

There are several ways in which the class can get involved in this method. The teacher may play a tape-recorded dialogue between a person with a problem and an interested listener-respondent. When the problem has been presented thoroughly on the tape, the teacher turns off the tape recorder and asks the class how they feel the problem should be handled. Another way to present a problem is to read a case history (real or contrived) to the class and ask for their suggestions on how the case may be helped. A skit, or role play, which focuses on a problem is still another way to give the class a springboard for problem solving. Finally, if students are open and supportive of one another, they may be willing to talk about their own problems and get help in class as the members try to find Scriptural solutions.

Some basic questions may be presented to the class for their consideration as they try to solve a problem.

- What seems to be the real problem?
- What courses of action are available?
- What are the probable consequences of each course of action?
- Does a course of action violate any Bible principles or commands?
- Which course of action seems to have the greatest Scriptural support? Why?

- Did anyone in the Bible face a similar problem? What did he/she do about it? What were the consequences? What can we learn from this?

RESEARCH

This method puts students to work finding information related to certain aspects of the lesson. The assignments ought to be made in advance of the class session that will deal with the research topics and students doing the research should know how long they will have for their reports. The research may take the students on a search through Bible dictionaries, archaeology books, commentaries, concordances, Bible encyclopedias, and Bible atlases. Or it may lead to interviews to determine people's attitudes toward, or knowledge of, some subject. Whatever form it takes, though, the research should be beneficial to those who perform it and also to those who receive the reports.

LISTENING TEAMS

Before a lecture or video presentation the class is divided into several teams. Each team is asked to listen for specific ideas, answers to questions, or solutions to problems, etc., during the presentation. For best results they should write down their findings. Afterwards, the teams share the results of their listening and interact with one another.

Obviously, this method is an attention-getting device, but it helps the students in a concrete way to derive helpful information from a lecture or video presentation.

It needs to be emphasized that methods are simply

teaching/learning tools. Just as the most expensive and versatile power tools depend upon a skillful craftsman's ability to use them correctly, even so the methods described in these last three chapters cannot accomplish much, if anything, apart from a teacher's wise use of them. The teacher of adults is the most important variable in this whole matter of teaching and learning. If he selects his methods wisely and employs them skillfully, his students will benefit immensely. He must regard methods as tools and not miracle-workers.

QUICK REVIEW

1. Buzz groups are formed from the entire class, meet in session, then assemble again as a whole class.　　T　F

2. The debate method doesn't have to follow an orderly procedure to be effective.　　T　F

3. For best results a debate should be held on the spur of the moment.　　T　F

4. A good summary by a moderator is essential to the effectiveness of panel discussion.　　T　F

5. A forum involves the whole class in asking questions of the teacher or guest speaker.　　T　F

6. A symposium uses more than one speaker and includes audience participation through the use of a question and answer period.　　T　F

7. In brainstorming, the class comments on each person's idea before moving on to the next idea.　　T　F

8. The project method is useless.　　T　F

9. Problem-solving can utilize a number of other teaching/learning methods.　　T　F

10. Methods are only as good as a teacher's skillful selection and use of them permit them to be.　　T　F

Answers:
1.T 2.F 3.F 4.T 5.T 6.T 7.F 8.F 9.T 10.T

10 How to Prepare a Lesson

The teacher stood before his adult class, confessed that normally he devoted each Saturday night to lesson preparation but last night had been different. A television spectacular had captured his attention. For three hours he had sat glued to the set. Only a brief interval between the spectacular and bedtime had given him an opportunity to prepare his Sunday School lesson. And even then his mind had focused on what he had seen on TV rather than on the Sunday School lesson. With that confession behind him, the recalcitrant teacher instructed: "Now, please open your Bibles to John, channel 4."

It was obvious to all that his mind was still feeling the effects of the TV spectacular, but there was nothing spectacular about his lesson preparation.

If a Sunday School lesson is going to accomplish something, it is going to cost something in terms of time and effort. Preparation must begin early in the week and be undergirded by prayer. This demands careful guarding of time, even to the point of refusing other positions in the church that would compete for the time that needs to be invested in lesson preparation. With early lesson preparation established as a high priority, a well-organized and effective lesson is just a few steps away. Let's consider each of those steps.

STEP 1: PRAY

As a teacher of adults, recognize that you are involved in spiritual warfare. You are battling against satanic powers that are bent on depriving you and your students of the blessings which come through receptivity to the Word of God. Our Saviour alluded to this malicious attack in His Parable of the Sower. He warned: "The sower soweth the word. And these are they by the way side, where the word is sown; but when they have heard, Satan cometh immediately, and taketh away the word that was sown in their hearts" (Mark 4:14,15).

Is it any wonder, then, that Jesus undergirded His own teaching ministry with much prayer? We read in Mark 1:35 that "in the morning, rising up a great while before day, he went out, and departed into a solitary place, and there prayed." Prayer, you see, is an effective weapon to use against Satan; and it is a powerful communication link with the Giver of every blessing.

Satan trembles when he sees
the weakest saint upon his knees.

When you pray, ask for clarity of thought so that you will arrange an informative, interesting and challenging lesson. Pray, as the psalmist prayed, "Open thou mine eyes, that I may behold wondrous things out of thy law" (Psalm 119:18).

Pray for insight to prepare the lesson in a way that will help the students to do their best learning.

Pray for a responsive attitude on the part of each student. If possible, pray for each student by name, asking that the student will be helped to appropriate God's resources and do His will. Pray, too, that the students will be edified in such a manner that they will be able to strengthen one another in all their relationships.

Pray for your own spiritual growth, asking that the lesson will grip your innermost being in such a way that you will be an appropriate model of the Christian life.

Pray that God will be glorified and pleased by your preparation of the lesson and your students' response to it.

STEP 2: READ THOROUGHLY

Read the Lesson Scripture carefully and prayerfully. Read the teacher's manual, the student book, and the additional curriculum aids. Read the related Scriptures that are referred to in the curriculum materials. Read at a comfortable pace, and try to get a feel for the grand sweep of the lesson's theme as well as a sense of what can be accomplished in your students' lives.

STEP 3: READ AGAIN, UNDERLINING KEY COMMENTS AND POINTS

This reading should be performed slowly, cautiously, and deliberately. Everything that was read earlier should be read again. As you read this time, underline the main points of the lesson as well as key comments and illustrations that explain and apply the Lesson Scripture. Don't be afraid to mark the curriculum materials in this way. Their main purpose is utilitarian rather than aesthetic. Put them to work for you.

In this step you should consult commentaries and whatever additional Bible study tools may shed some light on the Lesson Scripture. Again, underline what you find most helpful.

STEP 4: TAKE AIM

Aim for nothing, and you're sure to hit it. So, if you don't want to teach a lesson that fails to accomplish something, you need to select an appropriate lesson aim. Generally, curriculum materials give an aim for each lesson that can be used effectively. But you have the privilege of modifying the published aim. As a matter of fact, you may scrap it completely and devise your own aim. Since you know your students better than anyone else, you are in the driver's seat when it comes to planning a lesson. The curriculum publisher will not feel hurt in the least if you use his materials as resource helps instead of thinking of them as verbally inspired Scriptures that cannot be altered.

Generally, a lesson aim should have a threefold character. 1) It should be *factual*. As a result of the lesson, your students should know certain things. 2) It should be *inspirational*. As a result of the lesson, your students should want to do certain things. 3) It should be *behavioral*. As a result of the lesson, your students should do certain things. However, as I have emphasized before, don't make the mistake of thinking that every student must respond to Scriptural truth in precisely the same way. Appropriate responses to a passage of Scripture are as wide-ranging as human personality and levels of Christian growth are diverse. Perhaps the best reason for having a lesson aim is to give unity and direction to the lesson so that students will know what God's Word teaches and decide on an individual basis how they will respond to it in a way that pleases Him.

STEP 5: ORGANIZE A LESSON PLAN IN KEEPING WITH THE AIM

This step calls for weeding out and note-taking. Go

over everything you underlined in Step 3. As you do so, decide whether something that is underlined should be included in the lesson plan. How valuable is it? Does it serve the purpose of the lesson aim, providing important knowledge, inspiration, and the motivational bases for spiritual growth? If it fits, write it into your preliminary notes.

This is also the time to decide upon your teaching methods. Will lecture best help your students to get the maximum spiritual good out of this lesson? Or will discussion be in their best interest? Or perhaps role playing and brainstorming should be used. Maybe this lesson lends itself to buzz group format. When you decide upon the method you will use, write it into your notes. And indicate in your notes when you will use it — at the beginning of the class session, in the middle, or at the end.

You should also decide upon any audiovisuals you will employ in teaching the lesson, and identify these in your preliminary notes. At the same time, survey all the resources you have received from the curriculum publisher. Will you use this assignment from the student manual, or a different assignment from the student manual? Will you interject certain discussion starters from the teacher's manual or student's material? What about the quiz the publisher has provided? And will you refer to certain cross-referenced Scriptures given in the material? Well, all of these helps from the publisher are good, but you should make the selection of what you will use, based on what you feel is *best* for driving home to your students the truths you believe they need and want to claim. Having made this selection, make a brief list of these items for later reference.

Finally, if you want to add a poem, thought, or illustration of your own to what is supplied by your teacher's manual, consult your resource card file and make your selection.

Now that you have this material assembled in your preliminary notes, you are ready for Step 6.

STEP 6: PUT NOTES IN FINAL FORM

A blank sheet of paper measuring 5½ inches by 8½ inches (half of an 8½ by 11 inch sheet) is ideal for holding your final notes. By typing or writing clearly in abbreviated form (one or two words to introduce a thought or illustration, abbreviated Scripture references, reminders for when to interject a teaching-learning aid, etc.) you can get the entire lesson plan and content on the front and back of this size paper. And you will find that it will fit nicely into your Bible for handy reference, thereby eliminating the need to carry a teacher's manual or a stack of note papers to class.

STEP 7: REVIEW YOUR FINAL NOTES OFTEN

Once you have finalized your notes on a single sheet of paper, you can review them as often as necessary until you have the content of the Lesson Scripture and the order of your lesson plan firmly in mind. Now, with continuing prayerful dependence upon the Lord for His help and blessing, you are ready for a productive class session.

A BIG QUESTION

How much class time should a teacher devote to each lesson in a published curriculum? This is a big question. Some teachers feel that they should teach one lesson per week, thereby staying on the schedule set by the publisher. Others insist that so much material is on hand from their publisher, and so many teaching/ learning methods abound that they don't have enough time in a class session to cover everything in a published lesson. They prefer to stretch each lesson over two or three weeks. Is there a definitive answer? I believe there is.

In my judgment, a teacher should not spend more than one Sunday on each lesson in the curriculum. Too often classes bog down and become boring when even the best lesson continues for more than a week. But even when interest is sustained for two or three weeks, the teacher may be shortchanging his students, depriving them of learning how to study God's Word on their own. It really comes down to a matter of educational philosophy.

There are those who seem to believe a teacher must use everything he finds in his curriculum materials and corral all the facts and learning opportunities into the classroom, as though students pick up their "spiritual brains" upon entering the classroom and leave them at the door when they exit. Certainly, those who adhere to this philosophy would see a need to extend each unfinished lesson for as many sessions as it takes to complete it.

But there's another philosophy. It sees students as adults who carry their "spiritual brains" with them throughout the week. It doesn't confine learning to a classroom. And it views teachers as catalysts — motivators who make their students thirsty for personal, daily Bible study and closer fellowship with Christ. According to this philosophy, a teacher shouldn't think he has only 30-45 minutes per week to offer Bible learning to his students. Rather, he should regard each class session as a 30-45 minute period in which he can launch his students into a full week of interaction with the Lesson Scripture as they ponder its precepts and apply its truths to the situations they face. According to this philosophy, a teacher doesn't have to complete a lesson by stretching it over two or three class sessions. If it isn't fully covered in one session, the students can complete it at home and return to class the following Sunday for the next lesson.

So, teacher, don't be alarmed if you don't seem to have enough time in a class session to cover every point of the lesson. If you choose the right teaching method and organize your lesson plan according to the suggestions given under "Step 5," in all probability your students will get so fired up about learning what God has for them in the Lesson Scripture that they will finish the lesson on their own and emerge as better Bible students in the long run.

QUICK REVIEW

1. Lesson preparation ought to begin early in the week.   T F

2. Prayer is essential even to the most carefully prepared lesson.   T F

3. For best results a teacher must adopt the publisher's lesson aim without changing it in any way.   T F

4. A habit of underlining key lesson points and comments in the curriculum materials is worthwhile.   T F

5. Generally, a lesson aim should have a threefold character.   T F

6. Components of a lesson plan should serve the lesson aim.   T F

7. A teacher must cover every point in a lesson in a class session or else extend the lesson to the next class session.   T F

Answers:
1. T 2. T 3. F 4. T 5. T 6. T 7. F

11 Little Things Mean a Lot

What does it take to get an adult class off the ground? Really growing well, and giving men and women the feeling that it's absolutely the best class they've ever been a part of? Well, surprisingly, the teacher doesn't have to be an internationally known Bible conference speaker. Nor does the class need contest prizes like a 15-days, all-expenses-paid trip for two to the Holy Land or three days and two nights for the whole family at Disney World. It just takes little things.

A WARM WELCOME

A teacher ought to arrive early for Sunday School — early enough to shake hands with every adult who walks through the door. And with the handshake he ought to extend a friendly greeting:

"Bill, nice to see you this morning. How are you today?"

"Mrs. Jones, how are you this morning? My wife tells me your daughter in Seattle had a baby girl yesterday. Congratulations. This makes you a grandmother for the second time, doesn't it?"

"Ted, glad you could make it to Sunday School today.

That was quite a bout with bursitis you had this week. Feeling better now?"

Greeting each person in this way makes for a class where adults feel that they mean far more to their teacher than simply a few more numbers on the attendance board. Believing that he really cares about them as individuals, these class members will look forward to Sunday School each week.

Visitors should receive an especially warm welcome to the adult class. The teacher should greet each of them personally when they enter the classroom or he should appoint hosts and hostesses to greet them and introduce them to him and the rest of the class. Nothing is more inexcusable and detrimental to numerical growth than ignoring visitors. The Biblical counsel for winning and keeping friends applies to an adult class as well as to an individual. Proverbs 18:24a advises: "A man that hath friends must shew himself friendly."

Here are several ways to extend friendship to visitors:

1. Whoever greets visitors on behalf of the class should offer each visitor a cheery "Good morning" and give his/her name. If brochures or Sunday School handouts are available, they should be given to the visitors at this time.

2. Get the visitors' names straight. This means correctly spelled and properly pronounced. Perhaps the best way to get the spelling right is to ask each visitor to print his/her name on a visitor's welcome card. This card should also record the visitor's address, phone number, and church affiliation. If a visitor's name is unusual or hard to pronounce, the host or hostess should try to pronounce it and ask whether the pronunciation is correct. But no laughs should be enjoyed at the expense of a visitor's name, regardless of how funny the name seems to be! Remember, a person's name is almost sacred to him. Then, too, if a joke can be made of a person's

name, that person has likely heard it hundreds of times before and doesn't want to hear it again.

3. Introduce each visitor informally to others before the class session begins, or at the beginning of the session introduce him/her more formally to the whole class.

4. Recognize each visitor's attendance by giving an appropriate token, such as a carnation or souvenir pen. (An advantage in giving a carnation is that its clear visibility identifies the wearer as a visitor, thereby making it easier for class members to pick him or her out of the crowd so that they may add their words of personal welcome.)

5. Call on the visitors at home during the week. If the teacher is unable to do this, class members should do so. As a matter of fact, the more class members who assist the teacher with visitation, the more vital the class will be, both in terms of outreach and fellowship. The visits should be brief, friendly, informative and spiritually helpful. Those who represent the class should try to convey to the newcomers the fact that the class genuinely and earnestly wants them to return to Sunday School next week and become regular members of the class.

6. Create a spirit of hospitality among class members, so that visitors will get invited for Sunday dinner or at least asked to return for the evening service and refreshments at someone's home after the service. In a largely impersonal, uncaring world, this kind of thoughtfulness will mean much to your visitors.

7. Give visitors full information about special events. Most churches have traditions. It may be that on a certain date every year the adult class holds a potluck dinner. According to tradition, the potluck begins promptly at 40 minutes after the announced starting time. Also, according to tradition, everyone brings enough food for their family and uses dishes and

silverware from home. Tradition may also dictate that a committee prepares the beverages and the dessert. Unless the visitors receive the necessary information about when to arrive and what to bring, embarrassment could easily result.

They might arrive on time for the potluck, carrying hot food that will cool off before the potluck actually begins forty minutes later. They may not have brought dishes and silverware from home, thinking it would be supplied from the church kitchen. They may have prepared their own coffee and iced tea. And, consequently, they could decide that visitors aren't considered very important. So, to avoid discouraging and perhaps losing visitors, give them all the information they need.

SOCIAL TIMES

Having mentioned the possibility of visitors meeting with a bad experience at a potluck, I want to stress that an adult class ought to hold social times regularly. Adults need fellowship. They need to relax and enjoy themselves in the company of other Christians. These social times don't have to be elaborate to be enjoyable. A bowling social, a homemade ice cream social, a picnic at the park, a bus tour in the fall to view the leaves in their radiant hues, attending a basketball game — all of these occasions, and more, can provide opportunities for adults to build personal relationships that are rewarding. And in the process a great adult class gets built.

VISITATION

Not enough can be said about the importance of visitation in building a great Sunday School class. I have already pointed out the need to visit those who have visited the adult class, but regular class members ought to be visited too. As a teacher calls on the homes of his adults, he gets to know them better. They share with him their joys and their heartaches. He learns what their needs and interests are, and this helps him to prepare each Sunday School lesson with his students in mind. Then, too, adults appreciate a teacher who thinks enough of them to visit them. And that appreciation is bound to show up in better Sunday School attendance and a willingness to cooperate with the teacher in making the class an overwhelming success.

REMEMBERING SPECIAL OCCASIONS

Another little thing that means a lot is the teacher's remembering special occasions. It can mean a lot to students to receive a congratulations card or phone call from their teacher when the occasion is a birthday, a wedding anniversary, a job promotion, the birth of a baby, or moving into a new home. And when times aren't happy, during the loss of a loved one or when there is hospital confinement, for example, it means a lot to students to get a comforting card, note, telephone call, or visit from their teacher.

But how can a teacher know when there is a birthday or anniversary? The answer is simple, *ask!* At least once a quarter the teacher can circulate a sheet of paper among his students, asking for their names, addresses, telephone numbers, birthdates (month and day only, since some adults might be hesitant about letting the teacher know how old they are) and anniversary dates. The following illustration shows how to organize this information.

Name Address Phone Birthday Anniversary
(month, day)
1.
2.
3.
4.
5.
6.
7.
8.
9.
10.
11.
12.
13.
14.
15.
16.
17.
18.
19.
20.

Once this information has been received, the teacher may transfer it onto a large calendar at home. Week by week, then, he can look at the calendar to see who will be celebrating a birthday or anniversary.

If the class is large, obviously buying cards and mailing them can become rather expensive. In this case, the Sunday School may want to designate an amount of money for this purpose. Either way, whether the teacher or the Sunday School foots the bill, it will be money well spent.

Of course a teacher can't circulate a sheet of paper asking the students to list their hospital confinements or times of bereavement, so how can he know when these occur? Usually, in a small class such information becomes common knowledge rather quickly; but in a large class it may not reach the teacher unless he organizes his class into small caring units. A caring unit consists of six to ten adults who promise to pray for one another faithfully and to be aware of the special needs within their group. As soon as a caring unit learns that one of its members is ill, confined to a hospital, or bereaved of a loved one, the teacher is notified.

PRAYER SUPPORT

Offering prayer for matters that concern students may seem like a little thing, but it can mean a lot. Before launching into the lesson, the teacher asks for prayer requests, then leads the class in praying for each of these requests. At the end of the class session he may reiterate these requests and ask the students to continue to pray for them during the week.

PUNCTUALITY

I attended an adult class one Sunday morning when the teacher failed to arrive on time. Class members and visitors alike waited patiently for fifteen minutes before the teacher came huffing and puffing into class. I learned that this was not an unusual occurrence.

In another situation, a church service was about to begin, but a glance around the auditorium revealed only a handful of adults in a sea of youth and children. Where were the rest of adults? I wondered. I soon found out, as an entourage of adults, led by their Sunday School teacher, filed into the auditorium. I learned later that this was a weekly occurrence, for the teacher habitually seemed unable to find the "off button" until fifteen minutes after the Sunday School's dismissal time. In both cases, it was little wonder that class attendance was declining!

Granted, it takes some discipline to start teaching on time and to end on time; but such punctuality will be appreciated by adults, and a healthy class attendance will provide the evidence of their appreciation.

These are just a few of the little things that mean a lot. The dedicated and alert teacher can add to the list, and the result could well mean the difference between an average adult class and an outstanding one.

QUICK REVIEW

1. Without big contest prizes an adult class can't expect to be a growing class.   T   F

2. It is a visitor's responsibility to be the first to speak to others in the class.   T   F

3. Laughs at the expense of a visitor's name are not in good taste.   T   F

4. Visitors should receive full information about special events.   T   F

5. In asking adults to list their birthdates, it is advisable to request only the month and the year.   T   F

6. A caring unit consists of six to ten members.   T   F

7. A teacher should practice punctuality by starting and ending a class session on time.   T   F

Answers:
1. F   2. F   3. T   4. T   5. F   6. T   7. T

12 Self-Improvement Ideas

Without question one of the best communicators of God's message was the Apostle Paul. But this outstanding missionary/teacher didn't rest on his past record; he was always striving for even greater proficiency and accomplishments. Catch the spirit of the man as you read a few of his statements from Philippians 3.

> "That I may know him" (verse 10). "Not as though I had already attained . . . but I follow after . . . " (verse 12). " . . . forgetting those things which are behind, and reaching forth unto those things which are before, I press toward the mark for the prize of the high calling of God in Christ Jesus" (verses 13b,14).

This is the kind of spirit that sets a good teacher apart from mediocre ones, and compels him to keep on looking for ways to become an even better teacher.

For those who want to improve their teaching skills help is all around them.

FEEDBACK

Gaining an appraisal of our teaching strengths and weaknesses can be a valuable experience if we are truly open to constructive criticism. So it is a good idea to invite students to tell what they think could be done to enhance your teaching as well as what they like best about your present ministry of teaching. Naturally, students would tend to be more objective in an anonymous, written response than they would be if they were asked to offer their appraisal orally. So, a form like the one shown here, filled out at the close of a quarter of class sessions, can be most effective.

STUDENT CRITIQUE FORM

Please complete this form honestly in a helpful spirit. Your teacher appreciates your appraisal of his ministry and suggestions for improving it.

1. List the most effective aspects of your teacher's ministry.

2. List any aspects of your teacher's lesson presentation that you feel weaken his teaching ministry.

3. What improvements would you like to see your teacher make?

But students aren't the only ones a teacher can turn to for an evaluation of his ministry. He might ask the pastor, chairman of the Christian Education committee, director of Christian Education, his superintendent, or a fellow teacher of adults to sit in his class for one or two Sundays as an observer. Such a critique could prove to be a great help to the teacher as he seeks to improve his skills.

TESTING

Generally, tests are considered devices for measuring students' knowledge of a subject, but tests can also measure a teacher's proficiency. It is reasonable to expect most students to do well on a test if their teacher has done his job well. However, when students consistently perform poorly on tests, there is strong reason to suspect that their teacher has been failing at his job. So giving tests periodically helps a teacher to ascertain whether he is doing an effective job. If he sees by the test results that he is weak in certain areas, he can concentrate on improving in those areas.

IN-SERVICE TRAINING

If your church holds monthly or quarterly Sunday School staff meetings that feature in-service training, plan to attend these regularly. Even a good teacher can learn to be a better teacher, and every teacher needs the inspiration and comradeship that in-service training sessions provide.

SUNDAY SCHOOL CONFERENCES

Sunday School conferences are popular spring or fall events in most regions and are well worth a teacher's attendance. If you must take a few days of vacation to attend a conference, by all means do so. And if you must travel for several hours to reach a conference, be convinced that the conference is worth the long drive. You will be able to visit exhibits offering a wide variety of teaching/learning helps. You will be encouraged, challenged and edified by stirring Bible messages. And you will be able to profit from workshops that zero in on your teaching needs.

SUNDAY SCHOOL CLINICS

Occasionally, if a church is large enough, it can sponsor a Sunday School clinic for its teachers. Specialists from the curriculum publishing house and/or the Christian Education department of a Christian college or seminary can be brought in for a clinic and given directions by the church concerning the workshop topics the teachers desire.

If a church is too small to afford to sponsor its own clinic, it can enlist the cooperation of several neighboring churches. Collectively, these churches can organize a successful clinic.

EVENING LAY INSTITUTES

If you live within driving distance of a Bible college or seminary, find out whether it offers evening courses for lay people. You may be pleasantly surprised to learn that such an institute exists and offers courses in Bible and Christian Education. Enrolling in one or two of these courses each semester can be extremely beneficial to you.

CORRESPONDENCE COURSES

The better your understanding of the Bible, the greater potential you have for teaching the Bible successfully. So taking courses in Bible by correspondence can be very helpful. You may wish to consult your pastor for his advice on which correspondence courses to take.

ETTA

An organization of long standing and commendable ministry is the Evangelical Teacher Training Association. ETTA provides fourteen courses and two certificate programs, which may be taught by qualified persons in a local church or evening institute. If you have an opportunity to pursue an ETTA course, by all means do so.

OBSERVING OTHER TEACHERS

When I was a young teen and active in golf tournaments for youth, I met quite a few golf pros. Many of them were excellent golfers who wanted to improve beyond their present skill. They told me that whenever they played on a course where the resident pro was famous for a certain skill — driving, long irons, short irons, chipping, wedge shots, or putting, they would take lessons from him. It seems to me that even a good teacher, then, can improve his skill by *taking lessons* from other teachers who are well-known for their teaching skills. An apprenticeship, an occasional visit to such a teacher's class, or even a brief sharing time over a cup of coffee can be the means of deriving some good tips from an outstanding teacher.

BOOKS AND PERIODICALS

A teacher of adults who is serious about improving his teaching skills should surround himself with books and periodicals that deal with Christian Education subjects. A visit to a Christian bookstore will give you an exposure to these sources.

One of the most helpful periodicals providing practical help for Sunday School teachers is *Success,* published by Accent Publications, Denver. It is published quarterly and is available by subscription.

Your public library is still another source of valuable help for your teaching ministry. Although you are not likely to find many Christian Education books at a public library, you will find books on adult education, communication, and public speaking that can be most beneficial.

Teaching God's Word is the greatest privilege a person can enjoy, but responsibility to strive for excellence in the teaching ministry accompanies this privilege. Your determination to improve your teaching skills will lead you progressively to greater heights of effectiveness, and the Lord will take notice of this and reward you abundantly.

QUICK REVIEW

1. Only fledgling teachers need to attend in-service training sessions.   T   F

2. Several churches may cooperate successfully in organizing a Sunday School clinic.   T   F

3. Secular books provide absolutely no help for the adult teaching ministry.   T   F

4. ETTA is an organization that specializes in teacher training.   T   F

5. Asking students for their evaluation of a teaching ministry insults the teacher's dignity.   T   F

Answers:
1. F   2. T   3. F   4. T   5. F

APPENDIX

For those who use this book in a classroom or teacher training series this section provides study and performance helps.

CHAPTER 1:
FIRST THINGS FIRST

Think It Over

1. What conditions existed among the repatriated Jews in Ezra's time that made Ezra's teaching ministry so necessary? Do you see any parallels between those conditions and modern-day conditions? What does this say about the urgency of teaching adults today? What does it suggest should be taught today?

2. What constructive things might a church do to help its teaching staff to establish or maintain personal, devotional Bible study?

3. How does a teacher's lack of heart preparation hinder his effectiveness in the classroom? Should a church require

that its teachers of adults hold no more than one church office in addition to the teaching ministry?

Watch For It

Observe a teacher who inspires love for God and His Word. What do you see in his personality and teaching to suggest that he maintains a vital fellowship with the Lord?

Try It Out

1. Read the book of Ezra for situations in which Ezra's devotion to God's Word is demonstrated.

2. Take an opinion poll, asking at least ten adults how much time each week they feel a teacher should spend in personal Bible study. Average the times and share this information with your class.

3. Using this week's Scripture lesson, make a list of things God wants you to do.

CHAPTER 2: WHAT GOOD TEACHERS ARE MADE OF

Think It Over

1. What do you feel is a teacher's most essential characteristic? Why?

2. Do you feel a teacher can have the spiritual gift of teaching but not see any spiritual progress in the lives of his students? Explain your answer.

3. How do you suppose it is possible for someone without the gift of teaching to be a teacher of an adult class? Would you make recognition of the gift of teaching a prerequisite to assigning a teaching position to someone? If so, whose recognition would be necessary?

Watch For It

Observe a good teacher in his class setting. What indications do the students give that this teacher has the gift of teaching? Which characteristics of a good teacher, listed in this chapter, are evident in this teacher's ministry?

Try It Out

1. Teach a class. Afterwards, think about this experience. Did you enjoy teaching? Did the class show that they enjoyed and benefited from your teaching? Ask a trusted and knowledgeable class member to give an honest evaluation of your teaching.

2. Prepare five questions you feel a Christian Education Committee should ask every prospective teacher.

CHAPTER 3: ADULTS: A SPECIAL CHALLENGE

Think It Over

1. Adult classes are often formed on the basis of age differences. Do you see any disadvantages in this system? Any advantages? Do you think it is feasible to form classes of adults on the basis of educational background? Explain your answer.

2. To what extent do you feel social, educational, and economic considerations shape adults' preference for attending one class instead of another? Do you think it is unspiritual of adults to choose a class on the basis of its socio-economic makeup?

Watch For It

Learn how a church with several adult classes organizes its adults into these classes. What is the basis for assigning classes? Could the assignments be made in a better way?

Try It Out

1. Compile a *brief* questionnaire to give to an adult class that will determine the reasons why its members chose to be a part of that class.

2. At the beginning of a class session ask each student to write down on a sheet of paper the things he would like to accomplish for the Lord in the next five years. Organize the responses into categories and report the results to the class the following week.

CHAPTER 4: KEEPING THINGS IN BALANCE

Think It Over

1. Who is most capable of establishing appropriate behavioral objectives for a student — a curriculum writer, an editor, a teacher, the student himself? Why?

2. Can you conceive of spiritual growth taking place in a non-behavioral way?

3. Can a person lead a life that is beautiful to observe even though his theology is incorrect? Explain your answer.

4. What weaknesses, if any, do you see in appraising Sunday School lessons on the basis of how well they meet personal needs?

Watch For It

Observe a class in which there is limited attention paid to Bible content. What sorts of things go on in the class session? Are they constructive in helping the adults to decide an issue or discern truth from error or determine a course of action? Do you think additional Bible content would have made a worthwhile contribution? Why?

Try It Out

1. Ask students to write down their needs. Collect the papers and tabulate the results. See whether the needs are similar or wide-ranging. What do you learn from this about planning lessons based upon needs?

2. At the close of a class session ask students to write down how they will use what they learned from the lesson. Collect the papers and tabulate the results. Are the applications similar or wide-ranging? What do you learn from this about setting specific lesson aims?

CHAPTER 5:
COMMUNICATION BRIDGES

Think It Over

What sorts of things do you think act as barriers to effective communication? What can a teacher do to eliminate many of these barriers?

Watch For It

Observe two adult classes in contrasting environments — the one environment, bright and attractive; the other, poorly lighted and rather unattractive. Do you see any differences in the way the teachers perform? Do you see any differences in the way the students respond to teaching? Do you feel a classroom environment affects learning? Why?

Trv It Out

1. As an experiment in communication, write the word "strike" on the chalkboard. Ask your class to suggest the various meanings of the word. Possibilities are: a work stoppage, knocking down all ten bowling pins with the first ball, catching a fish, to hit an object, to light a match, a discovery of a rich mineral deposit, etc. Explain that because

so many words have different meanings, we cannot communicate effectively unless we understand the context in which each word is used. As a follow-up to this, ask each student to give a written definition of "salvation." Ask each one to read his definition. How much disagreement exists over this term that is used so often in evangelical circles? What does this tell you about the importance of defining terms?

2. Try using eye contact in a class session. Look directly at one person for a few moments as you talk, then shift your focus to another person, and so on.

CHAPTER 6:
THE TOOLS OF THE TRADE

Think It Over

1. How would you respond to someone who claims that a teacher doesn't need any books except the Bible?

2. What benefits do you see in curriculum materials?

3. Do you believe a teacher should follow the schedule of courses set by the curriculum publisher? Why?

Watch For It

Visit a Christian bookstore and see the kinds of books referred to in this chapter. Look for items that can go into a resource card file. Ask a successful teacher of adults to show you his filing system.

Try It Out

Start a resource card file by listing subjects on at least one master sheet and preparing twenty-five entries into your card file.

CHAPTER 7: TEACHING METHODS

Think It Over

1. What do you see as the greatest strengths and weaknesses of the lecture method? Do you feel lecturing is more suitable to young adults or older adults? Or do you feel this distinction can't be made? Explain your answer.

2. Do you agree or disagree that class discussion usually amounts to a pooling of ignorance? Why?

Watch For It

Observe a teacher use the discussion method effectively. What does he do, or not do, that makes this method so successful?

Try It Out

Lead a discussion group for ten minutes, having prepared two or three key questions for the class to discuss. After doing so, think about this experiment. What worked well? What problems, if any, did you encounter? What would you do differently next time?

CHAPTER 8: MORE TEACHING METHODS

Think It Over

1. Which method(s) would you use to teach a lesson on The Good Samaritan? Why?

2. How would you handle the complaint that skits and role playing have no place in Sunday School because they tend to

be entertaining?

3. Can you identify a passage of Scripture that might lend itself well to role playing?

Watch For It

Observe a skit or role playing situation in an adult class. Determine whether it enhances the students' interest and learning.

Try It Out

1. Plan a skit and present it during a class session, or —

2. Select someone to model some kind of behavior you feel your students ought to learn to perform.

CHAPTER 9: STILL MORE TEACHING METHODS

Think It Over

1. Think about the adult class with which you are most familiar; would the debate method be well received by them or would it turn into an upsetting experience?

2. Think about this adult class again. Are there special problems they face that could be treated effectively by the problem-solving method? What are they?

3. Which of the methods described in this chapter would you like to try out first? Why?

Watch For It

1. Observe a debate or panel discussion on TV. How is it organized? What role does the moderator play?

2. Observe an adult class in which any of the methods described in this chapter are used. What adds to their effectiveness? What detracts from their effectiveness?

Try It Out
In successive weeks try out a few of the teaching methods described in this chapter, perhaps in a team teaching situation. Ask your teaching partner to give you an evaluation after each class session.

CHAPTER 10: HOW TO PREPARE A LESSON

Think It Over
1. How does teaching Sunday School differ from all other teaching experiences?
2. What sorts of things do you feel are most helpful in a teacher's manual? What would you like to see added to curriculum tools?
3. How much time each day do you think you should devote to lesson preparation?

Watch For It
What goes on in a class session that stalls a lesson needlessly? What sorts of things does an experienced teacher do to keep a lesson on track?

Try It Out
Follow the suggestions in this chapter and prepare a lesson, organizing the lesson plan and notes on a single 5½-by-8½-inch sheet of paper. Practice delivering a lesson extemporaneously.

CHAPTER 11: LITTLE THINGS MEAN A LOT

Think It Over

1. What sorts of things does a class have a right to expect of the teacher between Sundays?

2. How many visitors have visited your class in the last three months? Did they receive a friendly welcome? Does your class have a visitors follow-up plan? If so, how might it be improved? How many visitors in the last three months became regular members of the class?

Watch For It

Be alert to special needs and concerns among your students.

Try It Out

1. Lead a discussion among your students regarding what they can do to minister to others through class activities.

2. Select one item identified in this chapter as a little thing that means a lot. Concentrate your energies upon making this work for your class in the next month.

CHAPTER 12: SELF-IMPROVEMENT IDEAS

Think It Over

1. Do you feel there is always room for improvement in even the best teacher's ministry? Why?

2. What skills would you like to improve?

3. Would you predict much success in teaching for

someone who is afraid to ask his students for an evaluation of his teaching?

Watch For It

Look for opportunities in your community or area for learning how to develop your teaching skills.

Try It Out

1. Select at least one of the self-improvement ideas from this chapter and pursue it as soon as possible.

2. Meet with other adult teachers and discuss the possibilities that exist for improving your teaching skills.

INDEX